WHAT IS A WOMMETT

WHAT IS A WOMMETT

MICK ABRAHAMS

Foreword by Bob Harris

APEX PUBLISHING LTD

Hardback first published in 2008 by

Apex Publishing Ltd

PO Box 7086, Clacton on Sea, Essex, CO15 5WN, England

www.apexpublishing.co.uk

British Library Cataloguing-in-Publication Data
A catalogue record for this book
is available from the British Library

ISBN HARDBACK: 1-906358-48-6   978-1-906358-48-8

Typeset in 11pt Baskerville Win95BT

Cover Design: Siobhan Smith

Printed and bound in Great Britain by
the MPG Books Group

Foreword
by Bob Harris

For a while there, in the sixties, it felt like Britain was the centre of the Rock 'n' Roll universe. Spearheaded by the Beatles, British music had stormed to the top of the charts all across the planet.

A young, exciting, new generation of musicians had arrived, blowing away the old order and grabbing hold of the music scene, taking playing and production to heights of energy and creativity we had never experienced before. In particular, the late sixties yielded a mind-blowing array of world-class UK guitar heroes who completely changed the perception of what the instrument could do.

Eric Clapton, Jeff Beck, Jimmy Page, Pete Townshend, Rory Gallagher, Alvin Lee, Peter Green, Keith Richards, Mick Taylor and others were taking their playing to completely new levels of feel and expertise.

Standing right beside them was blues guitarist and founder member of Jethro Tull, Mick Abrahams.

He made his studio debut with Jethro Tull on the album 'This Was', which stormed into the charts in 1968. By then, the band had become established as one of Britain's most spectacular live acts, with Mick's distinctive style beautifully offsetting the flute playing and wild stage antics of co-founder Ian Anderson.

'This Was' mostly featured music written by Mick and Ian, but the record also included the traditional blues song 'Cat's Squirrel' ... the track that did more than anything to forge Mick's reputation as one of the finest guitar players of a golden generation.

The book you are about to read tells the story of the curve up to that point and of the trials, tribulations and triumphs since ... a road trip through the life of a born survivor, through good times and bad.

Forty years on from those heady days of the sixties, I am

preparing to go onstage to introduce Mick and a host of special guests at his 65th birthday concert, to celebrate his contribution to British music and to acknowledge his continued dedication to the creation of great blues, country, rock and jazz influenced music that is both heartfelt and unique.

The sixties was a fantastic time. Today is even better.

Bob Harris

A preface explaining why so many stories and not so much about the music

Throughout the course of this book I have tried my best to be fair, truthful in my story and impartial towards friends and foes alike. You might think that I have been more concerned about recalling funny incidents and some (I will openly admit), hooligan-type behaviour from me and my companions and perhaps not enough about the actual music itself. Let me explain.

The music on its own spoke volumes about life in general from my point of view. I went through many changes as a player, a songwriter and a man. I have never been a self-promoting individual, a purist or a serious hardcore expert authority on anything. If what I do and play feels right and is done with good heart, then that's always going to be the greatest reward I could ever have. What has happened in the past is in the past. Most of what I did, good and bad (I like to think that most of it was good), was what it was. The bad things I am rightly ashamed of and do not condone in any way, but that's good old life being what it is and just that. The good things in music or otherwise I am rightfully and justly proud of. I wouldn't change one bit of it. The people who know what I am really like will tell you that I am still a big kid at heart and, although as I get older I can be a grumpy git at times, I still love and live life to the full. I intend to carry on doing just that; making good music *and* receiving and giving joy from the good fortune *with which* I have been blessed.

Mick Abrahams, 2008

Introduction
1975: Putting It *All* Away

There wasn't even the tiniest tinge of regret as I closed the loft hatch and put the stepladder back in its place in our garage. In fact, I was almost at the point of feeling quite numb about the whole thing... but maybe not quite yet. This, only time would tell.

I'd just put my old faithful Gibson SG Special guitar in its battered, world-weary case, left it lying up in the loft, and said: 'That's it, I've had enough of this crap. I want to feel normal again, even if it is just for a while... enough to give me some breathing space.'

You can probably tell by my opening remark that I too was battered and world-weary. I wasn't quite a case... but I was definitely distressed and at the end of my tether, not only with the music business but, sadly, with life in general. You might call it manic depression; personally, I'd call it a cluster fuck.

Since I was a young lad I'd had this dream of being a guitar player - and a famous one at that. And in this I guess I was no different to any other young ambitious kid, dreaming about the particular profession or calling in which he or she wanted to excel and become internationally renowned.

To some extent I had actually achieved that dream: I had been a founder member of the world-famous rock band, Jethro Tull; a founder member of the not-quite-so-world-famous, but highly respected Blodwyn Pig; and finally I formed what simply became known as The Mick Abrahams Band - and we even appeared on *Top of the Pops*!

But then for me somehow it all went tits up. Some of this was down to the way that the world is, whilst some of it, I well realise, was my own fault for not really following through on things that I should have. At least that's what some people have told me from time to time. In fairness, many of them have been right about some things, but most have been wrong about the whys and wherefores of what I did or didn't do.

Even so, each time someone did offer me another partial truth about my past I thought to myself, Hmmm ... You know, I feel a book coming on.

So, by stepping down that ladder from the loft I was also walking away from the music business in general and the rock world specifically. I'd had enough of the crap that had been dealt out to me by crooked promoters, cheating and thieving record companies, two-faced managers, precocious lying agents and, last but not least, shameless and very creative accountants who were as bent as they were outwardly respectable.

Even worse was the fact that the tax man in turn took it out on me and a few of my contemporaries. But he only did so because *he'd* been lied to by all of the aforementioned pack of wolves, and by anyone around at the time who fancied joining in the bun fight.

I do realise that that's the way the world is in all areas of life, but it always felt to me as if the arts, musicians and performers were looked upon as especially easy targets. Unless, that is, they were particularly clever and hard enough to take life's knocks; and – perhaps this is more to the point - were arrogant and smart enough to believe that they could beat the bastards at their own game.

Of course, some of them most certainly did. But having said that, nearly all of those people who did make fortunes and still have lavish lifestyles, have been the unhappiest and most miserable moaning buggers I've ever met.

Which is rich (geddit?) because somehow I've always felt that they of all people, being creative and not destructive should be made of stronger stuff; plus, they should be truly happy and able to put some true wealth back into the world - not only in terms of finance but in spirit too. Maybe I'm wrong on that one as well. Anyway, what I do know for sure is that by 1975 I'd reached breaking point.

So here's what I did.

I'd left the offices of Chrysalis Records a couple of days previously having told the guy who was half-heartedly managing me at the time (I think it was more *mis*management because I know he really didn't give a toss) that this was the point where I was saying goodbye to the music business I was hanging my axe up and, what's more, he could shove all the bookings and false promises as far up his arse as nature would allow.

His retort to this was: 'You dare to talk to me like that after all we've done for you? You'll never work in the industry again... you've had it!'

'Good,' I said as I gave him the finger whilst walking out of his office. 'If this is what you call an *industry*, I'd rather go and clean windows... so *fuck you*! And fuck the rest of you too!'

Now with the huge benefit of hindsight I do realise that the day I put my dear guitar away what I'd actually done was kick the cat – but not the problem. And this very same realisation maybe also serves as the subtext for my story. I'd like to think that this book is basically about a guy whose journey has taught him - painfully at times - how to always kick the problem...and never the cat.

But please judge for yourself.

Chapter 1
Me and Hermann Goering
7th April; the year 1943

I was born in a home in Norfolk for unmarried mothers on 7th April in the middle of a bombing raid courtesy of Hermann Goering and his lovely little friends the Luftwaffe. No wonder I still suffer with headaches! After a couple of days I was trundled back to my temporary home in Lowestoft, which was to be my family home for a short time. I am still not sure to this day who my biological father was. I have the distinct feeling that in those dark days of the war most younger people's attitudes extended to shagging everybody as much as they could and then sharing the kids out at Christmas time.

Needless to say that by the time November came around I was surplus to requirements and put up for adoption. I just don't think my mother could cope with the thought of having a kid round her neck and, from what I have gathered later in my life, she wasn't a particularly maternal kind of person. She just liked the practice part of making babies and not the responsibility that goes with it. I'm not being at all judgemental about her; but that's how it seems to me. Fortunately help arrived in the form of my adopted parents Grace and Fred Abrahams who took me in and gave me what was to become the best and most loving home that anyone could have had.

When my dear old mom finally passed on recently at the ripe old age of not quite 101, I did some research and it showed that my parents had their hands full with a whole load of trouble from my biological mother, who didn't seem to be able to make up her mind for love nor money as to whether she wanted me or not. So before I was finally adopted legally, there was a tug of war going on between the adoption agency, my prospective new parents and my biological mother. Fortunately my adopted parents Fred and Grace won the day and by November of that year I was ensconced in my new home in Luton Bedfordshire and this, folks, is where my story really begins.

Chapter 2
What a Memory!

You have to remember that in those days, there was a world war still raging and times were certainly not easy. I think, though, that people then were more resilient to adversity, perhaps far more than folks seem to be in these modern times.

My earliest memories begin at the age of 18 months. I vividly remember being pushed in a little blue four-wheeled buggy by my auntie Grace (she wasn't a real aunt but just a friend of my mum - I don't think we could afford real relatives at the time!) down towards Wardown Park, a local beauty spot from a bygone age which now sports such wonderful decorations as used French letters, discarded needles and various graffiti and, of course, the obligatory fast food wrappers tastefully scattered all over the place. Progress is wonderful, don't you think?

I was fascinated by a beautiful tree which for no particular reason I had named the "MMm tree". I think I was trying to say monkey tree as it was in fact a monkey puzzle tree, but that's just how it came out. 'MMm tree', I shouted with delight. Suddenly my auntie became quite agitated by a horrible droning sound from the sky above which I was later to discover was our old mate Goering and his group of funsters again who had now invented a new novel but deadly way of trying to dispose of the great British nation. Yes, you've guessed it; it was in fact a V-1 rocket, otherwise known as the doodlebug. For those of you who are not familiar with this lovely bit of equipment, it was a flying bomb. In this instance intended for the nearby Commer car factory in Biscot Road, Luton, which was just adjacent to the park and directly between me, my auntie, and the more rapidly moving pushchair.

What used to happen was that when the awful droning sound ceased, the bomb would then drop out of the sky toward its target and explode. By odd coincidence we were exactly outside the house where The John Evan Band took temporary lodgings when the first embryo of Jethro Tull was started way back in 1967. I'll relate this bit of the story in a much later chapter. As luck would have it, the bomb turned out to be a dud but it still dropped on its designated target and did some structural damage and I believe injured a few workers. Not half as much damage as it did to my poor old auntie's drawers though, as the experience quite literally scared the living crap out of her; there wasn't even an air raid shelter that we could have run to. I however was quite oblivious to all of this and enjoyed every moment. Why not? I still laugh to this day when I see someone poo their drawers, don't you?

Chapter 3
The Beginning of Innocence

I was a very impressionable child it seems. Then and still to this day my mind is like a sponge, just soaking up everything around me, enjoying what I like most and rejecting or ignoring the stuff that I don't. I think I must have heard so many different kinds of music as the family radio was always switched on and I can still remember Saturday mornings especially when Uncle Mac's *Children's Hour* was on. Such diverse and magical (to my ears) songs as Max Bygraves singing *I'm a Pink Toothbrush*; *Sparky's Magic Piano* (probably the very first special sound effect I'd ever heard); Burl Ives singing *The Big Rock Candy Mountain*; and a wonderful piano player called Winifred Atwell who, although she mainly played sing-along kind of music, was also an amazing boogie-woogie player. I think that dear old Uncle Mac even played a blues song every now and then just for good measure and, although I don't remember which ones, it must have had an effect on me somehow. I think the most striking thing for me was (and again still is to this day) great boogie playing. There is just something about that type of music that makes my heart feel glad and I want to jump up and down. Magic!

My next vivid memory was at the age of three and this is where the music all began for me. My mum was a piano teacher and as we lived in one of those rambling Victorian terrace types of properties which were quite large and extremely spacious, we actually owned two pianos. One was in what we called the back parlour and one in the front room parlour. There was a pull-down divider between the middle of these two rooms that could be pushed up into the cavity of the wall to make one grand spacious room and, as far as I can remember, it was always up for some reason or other. Anyway, it made for a great setting which I will always remember with fondness, especially at the Christmas gatherings of various aunts, uncles, assorted cousins and friends, where we would all sit round and sing popular song of the time whilst the coal fires in both parts of the rooms glowed brightly. It was a magical time for me.

As my folks didn't exactly exude wealth (my dad was a Vauxhall Car worker and not fantastically well paid) dad would always make me toys, such as a train that I could sit on made from wood with a large Ovaltine tin for the boiler, painted in the bright red livery of the LNER railways. It was a real treat and I took great pride in it.

Christmas time and summer holidays were the most magical and fun times for me and, just like most other kids, I never wanted those times to stop. Oddly even though both my sons are now men and making their own way in the world, that wistful feeling of never wanting it to stop still lingers with me and I look forward every year to Christmas and holidays alike. I guess I am still that same little kid deep down in my heart and I am not ashamed to confess it either. It's still a bit embarrassing for my wife when we go to pay the bill at a hotel where we've just stayed for a week and I start play acting and saying things like: 'I don't want to go home. I want to stay for another day. Please let me stay, please!' It usually raises a laugh from the receptionists when Kate drags me out by my ear whilst threatening to smack me round the legs if I don't start behaving myself. Me? Behave myself? You can't be serious!

We always took our family holiday at a place on the south east coast called Walton-on-the-Naze. It's a bit run-down now, but for me way back then it was the magic kingdom. All those wonderful sights, sounds, smells and the great feeling of being somewhere different from home. My oldest aunt (a real relation this time and my mum's oldest sister) owned a caravan and a beach hut there and we would sleep in the caravan and spend our days in the beach hut. The caravan was tiny and slept four people, so I had to sleep alongside my aunt and my memory of that part of the holiday was not good! She would snore and mumble in her sleep and fart loudly every now and then. I couldn't wait to get up and go over the road to get down to the beach hut and start playing on the beach. My aunt was a widow and another old school type disciplinarian, even more hard-line than my mum, so I was constantly getting ticked off about something or other for no good reason other than the fact that she was just a miserable old bat with nothing better to do than moan all the while. It didn't deter me too much however and the magic world of the seaside more than made up for any of the bullshit she could fling at me.

My dad taught me to swim at an early age and within a few days I could competently do some very reasonable impressions of a swimmer! The crunch came when I decide that I could jump off the small breakwater near our hut and ran the length of it and launched myself into the waves. In my young mind there was no such thing as danger and so I assumed that everything would be just like doggy paddling-type swimming near to the edge of the shore. Naturally it wasn't and my poor old dad nearly had a fit when he saw me taking my first potential journey towards the nearest casualty department of the local hospital. He ran after me and was about to jump in the water to fish me out. He needn't have worried as, although the initial shock of being underwater was pretty scary for a three year old, I managed to paddle my way up to the surface and actually swim to the shore. I had learnt to swim! That old saying about going in at the deep end is very true. It seems to have been the way of most things throughout my life and, in a lot of ways, I'm glad of those experiences.

As the years went by, we visited there every year until I was 14 and, with the passing of time, the music and entertainment that surrounded me changed with it. At the age of three and four I was hearing all the old crooners and popular singers of the day. Mostly American singers, whose records constantly belted out through the speakers on the pier day and night. Night time on Walton-on-the-Naze pier had some kind of special quality too as this was when the teenagers came out to play and it took on a whole different aspect. As a small child I was totally in awe of them even though play (you know the kind of stuff: playing soldiers in the sand, building sand castles and chasing seagulls) was foremost in my mind, things had started to click about what might be. Again as more years passed, the styles of dress and behaviour changed and the music had really started to change too.

One odd thing that still sticks out in my mind is about my dad. The poor man had a dreadful speech impediment. He stammered and stuttered constantly and to my way of thinking it was made all the worse by the fact that my mum constantly nagged him about it. Instead of being simply patient with him and waiting for him to finish a word or sentence that he was stuck on, she would nudge him in the ribs or shoulder and say very rudely: 'Fred: say your words properly!' This made matters worse and of course it goes without saying that this is not the right or kindly way to treat anyone with such a problem. It was compounded by the fact that my aunt Nell (the farting, nagging bat) joined in berating poor old dad too! I was always embarrassed and angry for dad about that and I learnt again later on in life that my dad had perfectly good speech capability up until a year after he was married to my mum! I don't know if there is any psychological reason why this should have occurred, but it seems suspicious to me. I try to be mindful of people's disabilities and to be patient and not patronising toward them and, at the very least, to be helpful if I possibly can. Although my mum's attitude seemed very harsh and uncaring at times, in her defence I have to say that she simply didn't know how to deal with it and I think was totally unaware that she was adding to the problem rather than helping. That was the way she was brought up and that was that. Still nonetheless annoying.

Mum, being a piano player, was always being called on to play at any social gathering (in our case mostly at Christmas) and she bought some new sheet music every year to play all the popular songs of the time. Of course there were many songs left over from the war days that were still popular and they were played and sung with great gusto by the assembled family. Songs like, *If You Were the Only Girl in the World* and Al Jolson's *Sonny Boy*, which for some strange reason always made me cry when my Dad sang it to me while I was sitting on his knee. It wasn't that he was a bad singer or anything; I think it was just the emotion of feeling loved and happy and at the same time never wanting the moment to stop. Oddly enough, many years later in my formative youth, the song *If You Were the Only Girl* in the World was sung by the late great Johnny Kidd of Johnny Kidd and the Pirates fame. I loved his version, and of course it brought back happy memories of those early years.

When I was four, my Mum started to teach me to play the piano and being a strict disciplinarian made sure that I learnt to read music and practise the scales. To be honest, I found it incredibly boring as all I really wanted was for the piano to sound like the songs that I'd heard and of course they never did. The fact that I was not (and still am not) particularly skilled or interested in mathematics (and thus musical theory) stunted my interest in the piano. The one thing though that I really got a thrill from was hearing boogie woogie and that I think was the real turning point for me, even at the age of five and a half. I was still to discover the instrument that completely changed my outlook on music and eventually the course of my life.

Chapter 4
The Hated Years of Education!

By this time I had been sent to Dunstable Road Primary School in Luton, which I took an immediate dislike to. I think the teachers also took a dislike to me as I was always in some kind of scrape or other and constantly ran back home. My dear old mum got it in her mind that her budding genius of a child would be better educated privately and moved me to a fee-paying school called Woodlands in Biscot Road, Luton. This was a menacing Victorian mausoleum run by two old spinsters who were so prim and proper you would have thought they invented the phrase "having a ram rod up your arse"!

These two old bats delighted in laying down such important rules as preventing mum and me from accepting lifts from kind parents who offered to take us home (we never had a car - simply couldn't afford one!). Total bollocks really and I still have no idea what their reasoning was. Amidst all the confusion of stupid rules and regulations there was, of course, some small amount of education (not music, I would hasten to add). I seemed to excel at English, Religious Education and French and absolutely nothing else apart from getting into trouble for one daft reason or other. I certainly never set out to make trouble, but wherever trouble was, it would be sure to involve me somewhere along the line.

I think my sense of humour was developed at an early age too. The traditional Sunday lunchtime was something I always looked forward to because an hour before lunch was put on the table, we would listen to amazing stuff such as *Life with the Lyons*, *The Billy Cotton Band Show* with Alan Breeze (a latter day big band singer) and my favourite, *The Goon Show*. That programme, apart from being the ultimate in silliness (the best kind as far as I'm concerned), was the very rock and foundation of all modern comedy and a lot of mates still remember all the shows and the favourite gag lines, like Bluebottle (Peter Sellers) asking Eccles (Spike Milligan): 'I say, Eccles. What are you doing down that coal hole?'

And the famous reply from Eccles: 'Well, Bluebottle, everybody's got to be somewhere!'

Evening radio was slightly more highbrow if you could call it that. Shows such as *Henry Hall's Guest Night* and *The Good Old Days* (which later became a television show), but the most exciting for me were the regular episodes of *Dick Barton, Special Agent*, which had a great theme tune and I remember charging up and down the room singing along to it "Dan da lan dan" etc. Great fun! The scary *Journey into Space* featuring Jet Morgan (the pilot) played by Andrew Faulds, and Lemmy, a crew member played by David Kossoff (father of the late Paul Kossoff). When we were able to get Radio Luxembourg there were shows like *Dan Dare Pilot of the Future* (a character on the front and back page of *The Eagle* comic for boys) and a music programme called *Cool for Cats*, featuring Kent Walton, yet another radio show that was adapted to television.

At the age of seven I was about to discover a new type of music that would open up a whole world of magic to me. I first heard the record *Cool Water* by a guy called Frankie Laine on my mum and dad's wind-up gramophone. I was absolutely fascinated. Wow! This was something completely new. Okay, it was a pop record of that time but it certainly had something lively about it.

I kept playing it over and over again until finally my mum

came into the room and told me to stop. The next great thing which was about to change my life was my ninth birthday, when mum and dad decided to buy me a guitar, a fairly beaten-up steel-stringed second-hand acoustic, which cost the princely sum of seven pounds and 10 shillings (that's old money to you!). This in those days was still quite a bit of money to shell out for the budding young guitar player. You see, they had noticed that I really wasn't doing that well with the piano lessons and was infinitely more interested in using an old string-less tennis racquet that I'd found in the air raid shelter at the bottom of our garden as an early form of air guitar. I spent most of my supposed practice time in the piano rooms (as I liked to call them) pretending to be a great guitar hero and gyrating wildly in front of a huge gilt ornate mirror that was hung conveniently underneath the divider of the two rooms. I seem to recall that by this time I had actually seen pictures of Elvis Presley and probably wanted to be him!

Chapter 5
The Start of Skiffle
and Rock'n'roll

At this time in history, the skiffle craze was upon us as a remnant of the trad jazz boom (which I personally didn't like, with the exception of the more blues-based songs). The popular artists of the day were the king of skiffle Lonnie Donegan, Chas McDevitt & Nancy Whisky, and Johnny Duncan & the Bluegrass Boys. So like many other kids of my age, I formed what was to become my very first band. We played at the bottom of the garden in my dad's shed and I, being the leader, naturally played the guitar and sang (the fact that I was the only one of us who had a guitar and could sing was really the deciding factor!) and a kid called Lennie from round the corner of our street played the usual improvised double bass made from a tea chest, a broom handle and a length of cord. Another kid played the jaw's harp. We always called it the Jew's harp, for no particular reason other than we thought it was only played by Jews because they were cheap! As for me I'm still saving up to be Jewish and so far all I've got is just the name.

For what it's worth, I'm led to believe that although Abrahams definitely has Jewish origins the name is quite common in Norfolk and Cornwall. I was brought up in the Christian faith, was confirmed, attended Sunday school regularly and was a choir boy and an altar server at our local Church of England (All Saints Church) at the top of our road and I think I enjoyed it far more than any formal type of education, secular or otherwise. Having a Jewish name, however, was quite useful to me as the road I lived in was in quite a well-to-do area in those days and inhabited by quite a few well-off Jewish families who for no accountable reason took me to their hearts and every Saturday morning I would visit their homes at the invitation of four families and in compliance with Jewish religious law appertaining to not working on the Sabbath I would do a very simple menial task, such as lighting the gas stove, for which I received the grand sum of sixpence. So with the pocket money I got from my folks and the few bob I earned being a part-time Jew, my life was reasonably sweet as I had some money in my pocket with which to buy the odd 78 rpm record. Bliss!

Chapter 6
Rock Around the Clock

My very first public appearance was at the suggestion of my dear old Uncle Harry, who was a committee member at the Royal Antediluvian Order of Buffaloes club near our house. In my imagination, I thought that they all dressed up as buffaloes and ran around the room for some reason! He was very kind and generous to me and always allowed me a sip or two of his pale ale when he poured one out in our kitchen and occasionally I would have a puff on one of his cigarettes (Woodbines of course!) He had been asked if my mum and dad would consider letting me play and sing a few songs for the members' social get-together one evening. Naturally I was very excited and quite willing to make my first attempt at performing with my new-found instrumental and vocal ability.

The only drawback was that I only knew four songs that I could perform with any great degree of accuracy - and that was mildly debatable - but as I always had the attitude of a true adventurer, I went for it. To make it seem that I knew a lot more stuff than I really did, I simply employed the old time-worn trick (I now know it's a time-worn trick but at the time it was a purely desperate measure!) of playing all four songs twice, but in a different order in two separate sets! The songs were *Don't You Rock Me Daddio*, *Oh Mary Don't You Weep Don't You Moan*, *This Land is Your Land* and the grand finale of *Rock Island Line*, although this was also the opener for the second set, but no one seemed to notice or care really. I got a great reception, whether from sympathy or appreciation I

16

don't know, but as far as I was concerned I had arrived. Yeah! As an additional bonus I was plied with pints of orange squash and they had a whip round for me and I received the mighty sum of one and sixpence!! Heaven! Fortunately, it became a regular Saturday night gig for a while and I even learnt a few more songs and additional verses to the existing ones.

My next aural memory was Bill Hayley & the Comets (our current bass player John 'Guinness' Gordon actually played with Bill not long before he passed away) and what an adventure that was. Until then the most exciting pop record I owned was Frankie Laine singing *Cool Clear Water* and Guy Mitchell's *Singing the Blues*. *Rock Around the Clock* was taking Britain by storm and it was featured in a movie called *The Black Board Jungle* which was quite a violent picture for its time about American high school delinquents. Glenn Ford played the lead role as I recall and the movie nearly caused riots throughout the UK. I think I'd also heard a few early songs from artistes such as Little Richard and Fats Domino and also the legendary Pine Top Smith. Strange really that, although the guitar was to become my weapon of choice so to speak, I still got that thrilling sensation down my spine every time I heard a piano played in that way and still do to this day. Little Richard's voice as well as his frantic style of piano gave me very much the same thrill and to me he is still the best. The lasting impression on my young mind was indelible: I had never experienced such exciting stuff. From that moment on the effect of music was expanding my consciousness about an entirely different world.

You have to remember that at this time I was still a naïve 10 year old whose view of the wider world was somewhat limited. In fact I was so truly naïve that I actually believed (mainly because Lenny, our tea chest bassist and fountain of all knowledge, had told me so) that a bastard was someone whose shit was green. I was constantly looking down into the toilet bowl after a bowel movement to check, as I was worried that I myself might well be one of the aforementioned unfortunates. I had no idea of the fact that I really was a bastard by definition of my birth and continued to believe this nonsense (much to the delight of my dear companions) until I was at least 12…13 years old, I think.

Still we continued down the skiffle road with our little home-grown barn band, but I was the only one who ever actually performed in public. Well, when you've got a residency at the Royal Antediluvian Order of Buffaloes Club the world is potentially your oyster, isn't it? The benefits of being in a band even back in those days had its fringe benefits as a girl of my age who lived in the house at the back of ours had a bedroom window which looked directly over dad's barn where we played. When all the other lads had gone home, as she had been listening and watching, I was treated to a quick flash of her naughty bits. Of course, being young and innocent (with virtually no knowledge of sex) I was amazed by the introduction to what could be best described as a free strip show for my benefit, (and presumably hers too!). Naturally I certainly didn't encourage this outrageous show of immorality. Impudent little hussy! Not bloody much I didn't! I'd probably by that time discovered the pleasures of the old five-knuckle shuffle even though I didn't know why I was doing it. But I bet I could have been a contender for the marathon by the way I use to run to the outside privy every time she showed me those things of hers. Ah, sweet innocent youth, eh? And it doesn't seem ever to have affected my eyesight as I was told by Lennie that it might. I just thought, sod it, I'll just carry on until I have to wear glasses!

Thinking back; if either of our parents had caught us

behaving like that we'd have both been beaten for sure, but fortunately we never got found out. Very sordid, but it did encourage me to read a lot more in later life, especially magazines such as *Health & Efficiency, Spick, Span and Razzle! Playboy* and *Hustler*, eat your hearts out! The stuff today just doesn't cut it like the old-fashioned soft porn!

Timelines get slightly confused when you're writing your autobiography. (I wanted to write someone else's but I've been told that mine might be a bit more interesting) so you must forgive me when I start to ramble a bit. Again I've always viewed the world through a pair of surreal spectacles and for some reason or other can't help but see the daft side of things.

On the subject of timelines; I have researched as best I can through a whole bunch of sources such as friends, colleagues, books and the good old Internet, so I truly hope that none of the artists, players and friends that have been such major influences in my life are offended by any mistakes I might have made about them and the time that they influenced me. I have relied on my reasonably good memory to put the events into chronological order as I've always felt that exercising the old grey matter is better than anything else. On the other hand, if any of you have been offended I am sorry, but bollocks anyway. I'm only human after all! I mean; what do you expect from someone like me? Charles naffin' Dickens? Tolstoy? Tom Clancy?

Chapter 7
School Teachers -
What a Bunch of Bastards!

School and music only ever mixed for me when there was a light operatic production or a carol service or some such extravaganza peculiar to the wonderful Secondary Modern school I had been placed in. Up until this point I had been expelled from at least two private schools for which all of the blame of my expulsion rests firmly on my own shoulders. The truth is simple: I bloody hated every single moment of every school I ever went to.

I only ever met a few genuinely kind and worthy souls in the teaching profession and the rest were totally pompous, jumped-up arseholes who seemed to have nothing better to do than knock kids about for the slightest misdemeanour, real or imagined. Like the wonderful maths teacher, Mr Sweebey, whose athletic prowess with a cane was legendary. His technique was a wonder to behold: he would bend the unfortunate boy over a desk at the far end of the classroom, take large strides to the other end and then run as fast as he could with the cane raised above his head in a manner that would have been a credit to a charging squaddie at Rourke's Drift about to do battle with the oncoming Zulu hordes! The cane would always land precisely on target (my arse!) at least six times before the sadistic bastard had had enough. Ahh! True education, eh?

History was always enthrallingly imparted to us by a rather rotund and powerful gentleman called Mr Mears who had only one eye. His nickname was Pussy Mears and he had a face that could be best described as a snarling beetroot with one eye on one side and a whelk on the other and a ridiculous mop of unruly red hair that made him look like a character out of *The Beano* comic. Why he was nicknamed Pussy; I never fathomed out as he was anything but. He made up quite adequately for his disability and fearsome facial characteristics by having an extremely powerful physique. His favourite method of teaching us about all the wonders of the world's history was what we called his right arm sucker punch, which he would deliver with incredible speed and accuracy to the upper extremities of your body. (I still think he was a bit soft hearted though as he always missed our heads on purpose!) And of course it gave us a wealth of knowledge of how to write about some famous event or battle whilst dealing with a completely dead arm or shoulder or trying to recover from a hard punch in the middle of your back. The slower you worked, the angrier he became and we would warn each other that Pussy was creeping up to deliver a crippling blow whilst shouting at the top of his voice: 'Work, boy! Work!'

Another sicko was our greatly talented art teacher, Mr Wally Walden, who seemed to be cut from the same cloth as the last one. His method of encouraging boys to draw and paint in a proper manner was this. If you made a mess of the work he had set you (and I usually did, as I couldn't draw or paint as well as a chimp in Whipsnade Zoo), he would make you stand in front of the class whilst he cracked you on both hands with a two-foot ruler. The real artistic part of his punishment regime was the fact that he always used the edge of the ruler. Sick twat!

Well if you want to teach people to draw and paint properly, you have to maim them first to prepare them for life's future prospects. His encouraging and witty catchphrase was: 'You've the brains of a fourpenny-halfpenny rabbit, lad!' Why he didn't go on the stage or music hall I will never know. That's not the half of it either. I think you might be beginning to get the picture why I hated school generally and resented most of the teachers that I came in daily contact with. Not all of them were small-minded sadists though. There were thankfully a few who had a true wish to educate and edify the youngsters in their charge. Mr Jones was our Religious Education teacher, and he was an extremely nice guy. For some reason or other I seemed to warm to his particular style of instruction, and I felt that he was one of the truly good-hearted guys at that school. The school itself was called Beech Hill Boys School in Luton, Bedfordshire.

We renamed it Beech Hill Borstal, which we thought was very apt... The first headmaster was called Mr Porter (or Percy Porter as we had nicknamed him), a seriously strict disciplinarian. When the whistle blew in the playground first thing in the morning we would all have to line up in our respective classes, just like being in the army, and he would stand in front to call us all to attention. Then he'd make us stand at ease and then to attention again. After he had enjoyed doing this a few times we would march off to our classes to begin the day's lessons. In some ways this was quite fun, as we could pretend to be soldiers. And of course some of us eventually did become soldiers. Very badly educated soldiers but nonetheless, good solid potential future cannon fodder.

Percy Porter's main concern for our education seemed only that we could all stand in line and to attention, I don't really have a problem with that, but there are other important aspects to life in addition to being able to imitate a ramrod! He was an extremely pompous and anally-retentive character who personified the type of people whose attitude I intensely dislike. He took pleasure in telling me that I would only end up in Borstal or prison or worse. I could have told him that there was nothing worse than where I was right at that point in time. The only time he ever came near to giving me a compliment or encouragement was when I sang and acted in my first stage production of *The Pirates of Penzance*. After the show, as I passed him, he mumbled, 'well done', but it sounded begrudging, as if he had been proven wrong and he didn't much care for the feeling.

A short time before I finally left that wretched dump, dear old Percy Porter retired and his place was taken by a more kindly and worldly man by the name of Dr Wharton Browne. As headmasters go he wasn't altogether a bad bloke but I think I'd already had my card marked by the outgoing administration as a troublemaker. And so I continued to get the cane every now and then for various infringements of the rules, like using the front door of the school to get to my house which was literally opposite, instead of walking round the two back roads from the rear of the school to avoid the bullies that were to plague my life for some time, as you will find out as you read on.

The canings weren't anywhere near as frequent as before, as this guy was not sadistic by nature it would seem. I think he was marking time before his retirement and just caned me to appease some of the sad excuses for teachers who still had it in for me from the previous years. I wasn't the only one, of course, who got picked on. There were a few genuinely bad lads at the place and they were regularly whacked too. I just seemed always to get roped in with the rest of them! All I ever wanted was a quiet life and I wasn't in the least bit worried about being caned by Dr Wharton Browne as before he gave you the stick he didn't do the perfunctory little tap on your arse to mark his whacking target and also to check to see if you were wearing any form of protective padding.

As I'd become so used to being caned for no good reason at any time, I had invented the "Abrahams Mark One Arseo-Tector", which I am sure with hindsight I should have patented. It was a simple arrangement of a metal worker's apron folded in two with a middle filling of thin foam tucked over the edge to dull the sound of the cane hitting your bum and of course preventing any pain. It was fastened round the waist inside my trousers with a large flat strip of elastic and I wore it nearly all the time just in case I was called out for punishment. Slightly uncomfortable, but very useful at times in my precarious situation. Anyway, when the new guy caned you, he really didn't have his heart in it like some of the seasoned veterans so it wasn't too bad really. As you're probably beginning to gather, school for me was absolutely a no-go.

Chapter 8
Death to all Bullies!

In addition to most of the teachers at this particular school being a complete bunch of uncaring morons simply waiting to collect their pensions, I was bullied constantly and mercilessly by three to four people in particular, whose names I won't include in this book as I don't want to glorify their nasty behaviour. The reason for the bullying was quite simple: I was the only guy in the school that had any real interest in music, and most especially any interest in the guitar, which was considered a bit of a "poofy" instrument. So every night on my way home I was subjected to various forms of bullying, name calling and insults, which I have to say didn't really bother me. But when it started getting violent - and it did quite often - it really made my life a misery.

I was quite a chubby kid, not very big and not particularly adept at violence. Unfortunately these guys were past masters at it and one of them made a regular habit of trapping me in someone's back alley and then beating the crap out of me. This was one of the very sensible reasons I had for trying to reach my home by way of the relative safety of the quick route front gate entrance as I explained in the previous chapter. This unpleasant pastime of theirs was always very entertaining for them and made them laugh a lot. Oh, what it is to be so popular!

Perhaps this was my introduction to entertaining, but not how I would have wished. Naturally the more I complained and showed weakness the more they did it. I even tried taking up boxing on the recommendation of my dad so at the very least I could defend myself from their unrelenting attacks. The boxing coach was a maths teacher called Mr Owen, a fiery, short-tempered Welsh chap who was as short in stature as he was in temperament. As I was pretty hopeless at mathematics, I think he already had the same lack of confidence in me as a boxer as he had in my ability with figures. However, he wasn't one of the bad guys in my opinion and certainly didn't knock the other kids around or cane them and I believe that he did have a bit of a spark about him that made him stand out a bit more than the others.

His nickname was Puffer Owen as the poor chap had only got one lung and smoked like a trooper, which clearly didn't help much. In fairness he tried to train me in the rudiments of fighting, but I think in his heart he knew he was backing a loser in this area. However, when the first time came for me to actually step into the ring for a practise match, it was with a very nice lad called Ron, slightly bigger than me, who was a very good boxer and had no wish to really hurt me. But, as luck would have it, I asked him just before we started, 'Please, Ron don't hit me too hard mate'. Sadly the next thing I remember was seeing a huge brown round object come hurtling toward my nose and the back of my head hitting the hard wood floor! I think I was unconscious for about two minutes, and when I woke up I was taken to hospital with delayed concussion. My brief but painful and embarrassing career as a boxer was over.

The bullying continued of course, as the callous combo had heard of my duff exploits in the art of pugilism and proceeded on a regular basis to bash me up whenever they could. There was a disgusting and terrifying incident when one of these heroes cornered me with a couple of his leery friends when I was playing near my house. This was truly the worst moment for me as I was nearly about to discover the unpleasantness of sexual abuse.

One evening whilst out playing with some of the local boys from my road in a block of garages just around the back of my house, I was cornered by the usual bunch of bullies that were plaguing my life. The other lads vanished very quickly as they were all too aware of the capabilities of this bunch and especially their leader's (and my main tormentor) propensity for sick and violent behaviour. What I didn't know up until that point , but was about to find out, was that this guy was not only a sadistic creep but also a pervert and an amateur rapist and he didn't seem to mind much one way or the other who or what sex. To say the least I was terrified as it looked like I was completely trapped. I pleaded with them to leave me alone but of course they loved that bit and so my pleas fell on deaf ears.

I was backed roughly and unceremoniously into a filthy, broken-down toilet which was adjacent to the garages and told that if I didn't suck this lovely chap's knob I would be slashed to ribbons with a cut throat razor! The fear that ran through me was unbelievable, but something just snapped inside me and I thought, no bloody way mate, and for the first time in my life I fought back with amazing ferocity and kicked the bastard so hard in the kneecap that he fell back into the wall and I was able to regain my momentum and charged like a runaway train right through the others and straight to the safety of my house.

The next day for me was totally unbearable as this guy kept coming up to me in the playground or anywhere he could find me and tell me what was going to happen to me after school. I could bear it no longer, I simply ran out of the school gates and went home in tears to my mum who tried to send me back (she had no idea of the trauma I had been subjected to and nor was I about to go into the sordid details!), but I wasn't having any of it. I played sick for a week after that and hoped it would all go away: the humiliation, the fear and all that goes with it. By this time I was approaching 14 years of age and realised that I had to do something to get my life straightened out one way or the other. There was a time that in my darkest moments that I actually considered committing suicide, but I think I was even too scared to go down that path. I can truly empathise with any unlucky soul who has suffered similar treatment and my heart goes out to them. At that point in my life I think I was more miserable and unhappy than I could ever be and if it hadn't been for the fact that at least I had my guitar to play every night when I got home I might well have ended up doing something stupid.

Chapter 9
The Awakening and the Reckoning

My salvation from a physical aspect was about to appear in the form of joining the Vauxhall Motors junior judo club. Now my dad had encouraged me to take up boxing to defend myself but frankly I couldn't take being punched, kicked and all the other stuff that goes with that sport. I was, however, quite strong and I had filled out a bit by then and grown in height. I found the exercise great, and the philosophy and technique of this form of fighting a very pleasant and enjoyable way of doing things. Judo means quite literally "the gentle way" and believe me when I say it's actually anything but.

What impressed me most was that the guys in the club didn't seem to be out to prove anything (that's except when there were competitions!) and encouraged the new boys like myself to behave in a more controlled manner and to channel the aggression into the right areas. The older guys who were the instructors had a good rapport with us young guys and we always felt confident and very well looked after in their care. The one thing that they - and judo itself - taught me was that in nearly all cases of aggression from another person, you use that person's anger, strength and balance to your advantage. From a philosophical point of view it taught me that all bullies are for the most part insecure and cowardly and do what they do because they have either repressed feelings or are, in some cases, abused people themselves and so all they are doing is passing it on, so to speak.

Personally I don't give a rat's arse what their reasons are. All I know is that some of these twats simply enjoy doing it because they are inherently evil, undisciplined sods and deserve whatever punishment they get. Nonetheless all of this gave me a new insight on how to deal with situations in a firm and positive way. In truth, when I got a bit better at it, I simply beat the shit out of the pathetic bastards!

I waited for my opportunity and cornered them on their own one at a time (bullies are not usually any good without back up) and the first one ended up with a broken arm (strike one for freedom loving guitar players!). The second one got covered in shit and bruises from me executing a beautiful hani-goshi (hip throw in English) on him into a huge muddy puddle (strike two for the peace movement!). The third one had heard about the other two's downfall and said he didn't want any trouble! (I still gave him a little dig though). And, as far as I knew, the last one moved away and was never seen since! The word had spread, and I was never picked on again. So all in all school for me was not the best experience in the world. There were nonetheless still a few decent guys at that school who I remember with fondness and got along fine with and who still keep turning up to gigs and concerts to this day and it's always a true pleasure to see them and their families.

I was by now a very good swimmer and, although I detested football and rugby and all the other team games, I owned an old Daisy break-action air rifle that my uncle gave to me way back when I was about ten and practised with it regularly in our long back garden in Luton. I was quite a proficient shot after a few years and was constantly accused of shooting at some old-fashioned clay garden ornaments, gradually an ear or finger at a time until they were finally destroyed. I was totally fascinated by guns and I am still to this day. In fact, I am a total anorak where firearms are concerned and have learnt to shoot many different forms of the sport over the years. I am constantly getting bollocked by my family and friends, when I watch a movie which has any kinds of firearms being used and I can identify models, calibres, types and how they work.

For instance, it really cheeses me off when I watch an actor firing a semi-automatic pistol which in reality would only have the capability to fire 13 rounds but they're either still blasting away about 20-odd shots without changing magazines or reloading or - even worse in my book - still appearing to fire the weapon when it has clearly run out of ammunition and the slide mechanism is in the locked back position. I hate bad continuity and usually make some comment or tutting sounds of disapproval and am immediately told to shut up! 'It's only a film, Mick,' they say, but these things are important to me and really spoil a good storyline. It's the old saying of spoiling the ship for a ha'porth of tar as far as I'm concerned, so there! Sounding a bit like Victor Meldrew now, ain't I?

Chapter 10
Learning Lessons

I really must be thankful that music and the performing arts kept me focused on what I really wanted to do in life. I think if there had been better teachers with a bit less of "up their own arses" attitude and a bit more love and care for the pupils as a whole, things would have been a lot better - not easier (I don't like easy things anyway) but more fulfilling and edifying. As I have grown older, my thirst for knowledge and learning in general has become unquenchable and I am sure it's because there was so little real education to be had in that place. As a result I now speak three languages and am currently learning three more, the fact that I was always good at English composition and grammar in general (again one of the more kindly and intuitive teachers taught that subject) has stood me in good stead.

Don't get me wrong here. I am all for good discipline and reasonable good behaviour and attitude, but I truly believe there are ways to bring that out in kids rather than just make them stand in line and march, sit down, stand up, and do mindless tricks better suited to a circus animal. All this time the music business beckoned and so, somehow, whatever job I took up after I left school I was destined never to be happy at. And the very first job I took was at good old Vauxhall Motors, where my dad had worked all those long years and his take on the whole thing was just to ensure I had a job, which was that of office boy and the precursor to an apprenticeship.

Well it didn't take me very long to get into trouble, as all I ever had to do was dress up in a stupid pair of green overalls and ride a bicycle around the factory floor with a basket on the front containing boxes of documents. When I wasn't doing that I would have to sit in an office staring blankly at the four walls that surrounded me. Almost like being in a prison cell; so naturally I would skive off and hide behind some large boxes and packaging and play cards and smoke. It wasn't long before I was caught and getting bollocked and cautioned became an everyday occurrence. Pretty soon, the cautions mounted up and I was hauled in front of the senior manager and told in no uncertain terms that if this behaviour continued I would be sacked. Oddly enough, this was exactly what I wanted to hear. So I continued! And sure enough, guess what? I got the sack, and that was before I even had a chance to become an apprentice.

Not unnaturally, my dad was extremely upset and who would blame him? His wayward son had entered the world of work, and within one year at set a new precedent for the minimum time of being sacked from his first job. I did feel sorry for my dad, because he had done everything within his power to ensure that I had a future, but it wasn't the future that I wanted. The next move was to become a grocer's errand boy. I got another free bike, but this time the overalls were a nicer colour.

For a while I was employed as a van boy/driver's assistant at the local Corona soft drinks factory in Luton and it was quite fun, especially as some of the drivers used to let us lads drive the ten-ton trucks that we had for supplying the local shops with the heavy one-dozen crates of Corona bottles. Every Saturday morning we would do a country village run and as most of the shops were fairly near each other the driver would just say: 'Go on, lad, get your arse up there and drive the truck up to the next shop. Amazing! A sixteen year-old kid in charge of a ten-ton lorry! In those days the trucks were a heck of a lot different to today's modern counterparts (they're luxury limousines by comparison). No synchromesh gearboxes so you had to do a thing called double clutching and de-clutching just to change the gears up and down (they were called crash gearboxes and that's just the sound they made if you timed changing the gears wrongly). There wasn't such a thing as power steering, no power assisted braking and certainly no flashing indicators either, so all indication and signalling was done by hand.

All-in-all it was a great learning experience, even though I was breaking the law by not being old enough to drive a car let alone a ruddy great big heavily-loaded truck. I absolutely loved it and I think it stood me in good stead for passing my driving test, which I accomplished the very first time at two o'clock on the afternoon of my seventeenth birthday, the same day that I received my provisional driving licence.

When I had completed the test, the examiner looked at me very oddly and said with a sly grin: 'I'm happy to tell you, Mr Abrahams, that you have passed the test and are now a fully qualified driver. Just one question I have for you though. I have just noticed that today is your seventeenth birthday' (which at the time was the legal age you were allowed to have even a provisional driving licence) 'and I am frankly very impressed with the fact that you must be either a magician or an incredibly quick learner to have acquired such good road skills and driving ability within the space of one morning. Have you driven before today?'

'Yes,' I lied. 'I have driven my dad's car around a disused airfield every week for the last few months and I took a three-hour lesson with the British School of Motoring this morning.'

My nose should have grown about four inches really as my

Dad couldn't even afford a car let alone drive one and the truth was that I did have a lesson with British School of Motoring for about an hour in an old-style Ford Anglia (the one with the weird sloping back window) and it was an absolute doddle to drive as it had light steering, indicators, a synchromesh gear box that you could change gear in one action. Even the driving instructor was really impressed, but for me it was a piece of cake. The examiner just smiled and said: 'Well done, lad. I think you must have just broken a record.' He knew I was telling fibs but, as far as he was concerned, I was a good driver and deserved the pass so that was it!

Within a few months I'd saved up around ten pounds from my job and bought a beaten-up second-hand Ford Prefect van which the previous owner just couldn't wait to get rid of. You didn't need such a thing as an MOT in those days, insurance for third party only was about a fiver and some naughty people used to put Guinness beer labels in the front windscreen because they actually looked like the current version of a tax disc. I might have done that once, but I can't really remember properly! Anyway the old van smoked and creaked, it had no proper back windows as it had previously been used as a builder's van, but it started (most times) and got me from A to B. All I did was to put thin plywood strips in the holes where the back windows used to be bought a couple of cans of spray paint from the local hardware store and presto: the first Abrahams-mobile. Yeah!

Chapter 11
The Fabulous Futurama Guitar and the Front Room Band

I just couldn't wait to get home every night and practise my guitar. By this time I had saved up enough money to buy an electric guitar: a Futurama with three pickups. This particular guitar had an extremely strange setup. Its lead had at one end a normal jack plug, which of course plugs into the amplifier, but at the other end there was a strange device in the shape of a co-axial plug, very much like the type that you used to plug into the back of a television set. When I purchased this guitar from a local shop in Luton there was another kid with his mother in the shop at the same time as me. He purchased an identical guitar.

A week later, I was back in the shop for some reason and who should be in there at the same time, but the same kid and his very irate mother. This time, the kid's left hand was completely bandaged and his mother was complaining bitterly to the sales assistant about the dangers of electric guitars. In a very loud voice she proclaimed that her poor little Johnny had sustained severe injuries from this terrible instrument of torture, which she had bought him in good faith. The sales assistant was completely flustered and very puzzled.

'What injuries are you talking about Madam?' asked the lady.

'These injuries,' said the mother and proceeded to unwrap the bandage around poor little Johnny's hand to reveal six bright red burn marks across his hands and the tops of his fingers. 'There,' she said triumphantly. 'What do you think of this? Don't you think it's dangerous to sell people such stuff?'

The sales assistant could not understand what had happened and asked the lady what kind of amplifier little Johnny had plugged the guitar into.

'Amplifier?' said the lady. 'What do you mean, amplifier? It's an electric guitar, isn't it?'

'Yes of course it is,' said the sales assistant, 'but you need an amplifier to plug it into otherwise you won't hear anything.'

'Well no, he hasn't got one of those,' said the irate mother. 'I've already spent enough money on the guitar!'

Oh yes, my friends, you might have guessed what happened. Yes, that's right, you've got it, clever little Johnny somehow managed to unravel the coaxial part of the cable and attach it to a three pin plug and plug it directly into the wall. The mind boggles when I think about this, as in a later chapter I will tell you exactly how I became a victim to what we in the trade know as the blue overcoat syndrome. I know I shouldn't have laughed but I did and I still do, stupid little bugger!

On the subject of guitars. I did at one time have an Arnold Hoyer full bodied f-hole acoustic with a DeArmond pick-up attached to the body by means of sticky tape. It was an odd arrangement and it had a wire dangling down which I had jury rigged to fit into the back of the family radio. Naturally, when I used it like this it was always blowing the speakers, much to the anger of my parents and as a consequence I was banned from using the radio!

Chapter 12
The Front Room Band

Anyway, there I was with my wonderful new black-and-white Futurama, and I started to play with a couple of other guys in their front room every Sunday morning. I had by this time graduated to an Elpico four-watt amplifier, which was heaven. We had a lead guitar player whose name was Johnny Sear (nicknamed Boda), a bass player, whose name was Dave Cakebread (later to become the bass player of the Toggery Five) and of course good old me on rhythm guitar, if my memory serves me correctly. We played about every number that the Shadows had recorded and probably a few Elvis and Chuck Berry numbers too. Only problem was that we were never destined to do anything but practise in John's front room.

It was fun and I couldn't wait for Sunday mornings to come around and spent all week practising to play like Bruce Welch, the Shadows rhythm guitarist. A couple of years before the advent of the Shadows I did try to play a little bit of lead as well and I will always remember the very first guitar riff of a song called *Raunchy*, a big swing band number by the Ted Heath Orchestra which was the B side of *Swingin' Shepherd Blues* recorded in 1958. I wasn't fond of the A side but wow! did that guitar riff stand out in my mind? I seem to remember watching a TV interview with George Harrison who said that it was also one of the first things he learnt on guitar and apparently he played it to John Lennon, which got him the job with the Beatles. It was only eight notes, repeated often during the song, but it certainly had an undeniable character about it, plus it was pretty easy to play. It was originally written and played by a guy called Bill Justis, but on Ted's recording I am not sure if it was played by Judd Proctor or someone else of that era and to date I have not come up with accurate info.

The other easy-to-play piece of lead guitar work was *You're So Square* by Cliff Richard and the Drifters, which was more notes to play - 14 to be precise - but it was still very easy as all you had to do was play the open E string and hammer it on and off at the open E and F position. Simple but very effective and it definitely impressed a few people into thinking you could actually play lead guitar!

I haven't covered the subject of work during this time, but I must have had about 25 different jobs during these early years as there was plenty of labouring work on building sites and in those days when one job either finished or just got too tedious or whatever, you simply asked for your cards or P45 as it was known then and walked up the road to the next building site or project and started there and then. Easy as that. Never any shortage of work for donkeys and no health and safety bullshit! All they needed you for was to hump, dig, lift and fetch and carry and I knew how to drive so I could drive the heavy dumper trucks for hauling concrete and bricks and the like. It was easy, reasonably healthy and always loads of fun, with good natured mickey-taking out of each other all the time so no rocket science required.

I loved working with a lot of the Irish guys and first generation West Indians that seemed to fill out Britain's main labour force in those days. I got on especially well with the Irish lads and for some strange reason being around them was good for my morale as my nickname had now become Big Blondie. 'How's she cutting, Big Blondie there?' was a common greeting, and just like the honorary Padraig I had become in their eyes, I would reply in a mock Tipperary accent: 'Oh, she's slicing just noicely now, wouldn't y'know!' Being the kind of character that I was developing into it was another form of learning for me as I took on board all the various accents and mannerisms of the different guys that I was working alongside. It certainly developed my mimicry skills and thirst for learning languages and how other folk from different countries and cultures behaved and interacted with each other. It was definitely good enough for me; I always had plenty of cash (as that's how you got paid) and no worries in that area.

Music, of course, was still my main priority. The rest to me was incidental and a means to an end, but great fun nonetheless. I remember going home after a day's hard graft and after getting washed and having my tea, sitting in my bedroom for the rest of the evening practising the guitar. With my hard-earned cash I had by now achieved the ultimate status purchase of a Dansette Major electric multi-play record player. This wonderful machine could play the old-fashioned 78 rpm records, which were beginning by this time to go out of fashion in favour of the more modern seven-inch and 12-inch long-playing records. It had a reversible stylus or needle so that it could play either type of record. It also played the small 45rpm singles and EPs (or extended play) records which usually had about four tracks on them. I would sit in my room with whatever latest record I had acquired and proceed to learn the guitar parts and bits of solos by playing them over and over again.

Later on down the line I had the pleasure of talking to Hank Marvin when we bumped into each other at a trade show in London where I was demonstrating Yamaha guitars. We had a cup of tea together and a long chat about the old days and one of the subjects I touched one was this thing about how our individual methods of learning songs differed. I was surprised to find out that, just like me, he and nearly all the other musicians of my era learnt in more or less the very same way. The amusing part was when Hank asked me if as a young up and coming player I learned to play the mistake as well. I was puzzled and so he explained to me that as the older type of recording machines in the late fifties and very early sixties only had the capability to record two tracks or in some cases only just one. The band or artiste had to do it all in one take as it was extremely costly to re-do the whole thing and there was no facility to do what is known as a drop in or edit. Time was money and you just had to get it right. Very occasionally there would be a tiny mistake made during the course of the song and if it wasn't absolutely glaring it would simply be left as it was, mastered and pressed and put out on sale!

His point was this. There were a few of those small but not too obvious mistakes left on a lot of the old fifties and sixties recordings, so as we were learning them we more or less copied them note for note within the limits of our respective capabilities. And although we didn't know it at the time we were actually playing the mistake as well! Sometimes these mistakes or bloopers were quite melodic and even musical little moments so it didn't really matter all that much. Just as long as you got the right feel of the song it was cool! I've done it a couple of times myself quite purposely when recording to see if anyone else who covered a song that I'd done would play the "mistake" as well and, sure enough, I've heard it for myself when I listened to a band who covered a Blodwyn Pig number and they actually played my "mistake" too! Fortunately it was a pretty good little musical mistake and it fitted into the song OK but if you listen closely it's there! No I'm not going to tell the name of the song or the band that covered it, so you'll just have to go out and buy some Blodwyn Pig albums! Good sales pitch though, isn't it? Thanks, Hank, I am forever in your debt, mate!

Chapter 13
The Advent of the Hustlers

After a while, we were fed up with the front room and moved on to greater things. The bass player, Dave, and I recruited a new guitar player. His name was Brian Taylor and he certainly had all the Shadows licks off to a T! We then met up with a guy called Pete Kemp, a rather big and not particularly good-looking lad, but who had a really good voice. At the time, he was looking for a band to join and he had a friend called Ray Dennis who was around the age of 40 but wouldn't admit it. He was a jazz drummer really, or a big-band, swing type of drummer, but I think for the sake of just feeling a young man again, joined the band. He immediately suggested that we should be dressed properly in smartly pressed trousers, white shirts and Shadow bows and of course that we should do a proper presentation when we played. I soon learned that he was once a member of the Royal Military Police and was a stickler for all things, "proper and military fashion" but he was a decent guy nonetheless.

I think it was just that he was slightly out of his depth with a bunch of less experienced, younger guys who really only wanted to play Shadows' music and rock'n'roll. We weren't actually that bad for a bunch of complete amateurs and, although Ray was probably the most experienced, we certainly could all hold a good tune, so to speak! We even practised the Shadows choreographed footwork which was to become their trademark as well as their great style of music. Our first paid gig was at a wedding in the village hall at Little Gaddesden, Herts, and I remember that we only had a repertoire of around 14 songs and instrumentals in all and that we had to play the same batch of tunes back to front in order to play three one-hour sets. The good thing was that no one really noticed as by the time the first set had ended they were all pissed and couldn't give a toss. And neither did any of us, as we were all pissed (with the exception of Ray) as well!

We started getting quite a few gigs locally and started making a bit of a reputation for ourselves. We called ourselves the Jesters originally and our band uniforms consisted of multi coloured mohair jumpers and grey trousers but, as I mentioned earlier, Ray Dennis the drummer was really insistent that we started wearing proper band uniforms, so the smartly pressed trousers, white shirts, black blazers and Shadow bows came to pass. For some reason or other we started getting gigs at local USAF air bases and these were to prove very popular with the military personnel, mostly what was commonly known as "other ranks up". One night, however, we were booked into the officers' mess, and that turned out to be a whole different ball game. Within 10 minutes of us starting, a very large and irate officer - a full colonel I believe - came storming up to the stage and told us in no uncertain terms to pack up our guitars and amps and - these were his words and I will never forget them: 'Stop that goddam noise and get the fuck out of my mess, you long-haired, ugly bunch of cocksuckers!' Charming! A true officer and a gentleman, eh? 'Take your money, and we never want to see you again.'

Now comes the really funny part. As we're walking out of his mess a Flight Sergeant from the NCOs' mess across the road came up to us and said: 'Seeing as now you guys ain't doing anything, how would you like to come across the road and play for the guys who do all the real work around here?'

Well, what could we say? We simply trundled our amps and guitars into *his* mess hall, set up and started playing. We went down an absolute storm, and we got paid double the amount that we would have got if we continued playing in the officers' mess. Bloody officers, eh? What do they know? Fuck all!

Chapter 14
The Royal Artillery.... Gunner
2265???? Abrahams

At some stage in this book I feel I must relate the story of my time in the army. Our lead guitar player, Brian Taylor, was already a member of the local Territorial Army Regiment, namely the Beds and Herts Yeomanry Royal Artillery 206 p battery. And I have to say I was impressed to say the least. Number one reason being that it seemed quite easy for him to pull birds because he'd got a smart khaki uniform with a few badges and nice looking accessories. Well I thought I think I'd like to have some of this, and at the ripe old age of 17 years I presented myself to the local recruiting office signed a piece of paper, and within three weeks I became Gunner whatever my army number was: Abrahams. I seem to remember it started with 2265 but the rest of it I am unsure about and, although I have tried very hard to find the absolute correct information, there seem to be no records going back that far for TA personnel! They really didn't ask me too many questions except, was I in good health? Was I reasonably fit? Would I be prepared to serve my country? And would I like to go off to foreign parts of the world and shoot people? I immediately replied yes, and didn't tell them the real reason that I wanted to join which of course was that I wanted to pull birds just like Brian. Anyway they gave me a medical examination which was very cursory and told me I was A1 fit, sent me off for basic training to a strange place in Oswestry, Shropshire, called Park Hall School of Gunnery.

We had to do all sorts of weird things toward whatever

impending war effort was needed (I think Archbishop Makarios of Cyprus was causing some sort of trouble at the time, so that would have been the exotic place we would have been sent to) such as running around a camp shouting silly things, running through lots of obstacles and other crap, being called the most foul names by our instructors and generally going to bed at night feeling totally knackered and not particularly looking forward to the next day. Now, being in a territorial regiment is somewhat different to being in a regular regiment for the very simple fact that the regulars look down on you as STABS: Stupid TA Bastards! Well, I ask you? We were doing just the same as them except we got crap equipment and they got the better uniforms, the better guns, better training and far better toys to play with and guess what? More birds than you could wave a shitty stick at.

After we had done all the running around getting covered in shit and generally being abused we were sent home to report every week to our local TA drill hall, where we would learn the fine nuances of dry firing the 4.2 mortar. These were the smallest guns that the Royal Artillery had at that time, which was probably why they let mugs like us play with them! They also taught us how to dry fire a .303 rifle and a .303 Bren gun, a very accurate machine gun which was the battery's main protection (or section weapon as it was known) should any of us be attacked from the rear whilst playing with our weapons. Ooer missus! Of course this was a particularly heavy weapon and they usually chose the biggest guy (or the mug) to carry the ruddy thing. Which in this case was me or "Wommett" as I was fondly nicknamed by our friendly Regimental Sergeant Major.

I did tell them, of course, I was a musician and a guitar player, but the minute I mentioned the word 'music' the only job I was ever offered in a serious way was moving the piano around the NAAFI. A Wommett, according to our erstwhile WO2 or Regimental Sergeant Major, was a strange creature whose attributes I will now describe to you. Sergeant Major Cannon (yes, it really was cannon!) when he was in a particular strop because I had displeased him would make me stand to attention with his nose quite literally two inches from mine, and pass on to me these memorable words of wisdom delivered in a loud, high-pitched screaming voice, with flecks of spittle and foam emanating from his mouth.

'Gunner Abrahams,' he would yell. 'You are a wommett, lad. Do you know what a wommett is, you manky excuse for a Gunner?'

'No sir,' I'd reply.

'A wommett, lad, is two pounds of shit, stuffed into a one pound bag, a belt round the middle, filthy rotten boots, dirty brass, unclean cap badge, rusty weapon, having the fucking audacity to be masquerading as one of Her Majesty's soldiers! Stand still when I'm talking to you,' he would scream. 'You're waving about like a fucking palm tree in the breeze.'

One fine early morning I was learning how to drill with the fabulous and very accurate 303 calibre Lee Enfield bolt action rifle which, even though I say it myself, I was rather good with.

'Have you cleaned your weapon?' he enquired in a more even tone (I knew what was coming; this was the lull before the storm!).

'Yes sir,' I yelled at the top of my voice.

'Present! he ordered. This meant that I had to bring the weapon up to the port position and pull the firing bolt mechanism back for him to inspect.

He then went into overdrive with the tirade, and the voice got a pitch higher and twice as loud. 'You call that clean?' I just kept my eyes front at this point and said nothing for fear of either being put on a charge for either speaking out of turn or dumb insolence (you couldn't win so it was best to keep your gob shut).

'You call that clean?' he repeated, 'that is the filthiest weapon I have ever had the fucking misfortune to set my eyes on. There are great big lumps of shit, spiders and couples dancing the tango up that barrel. Clean it you horrible man!'

One weekend we were practising live firing of the Lee Enfield .303 calibre rifle at Grafam Waters Ranges and had just trudged across the muddy field to our designated part of the range. We had been issued with about 50 rounds of .303 ammunition each. There were ten of us at one time all lying down on our front and preparing to fire the first five rounds from the prone position at a static target a hundred yards down the range.

The small arms gunnery sergeant instructor had given us the order to load and prepare to fire on his command five rounds "rapid snap", as it was called. The Lee Enfield Mark One Number Four rifle is an extremely accurate and reliable weapon in the right hands and has a small magazine located directly underneath holding ten rounds loaded in two strips of five from the top of the weapon. All you had to do to make the weapon ready to fire was, after pushing the rounds in through the supplied stripper clip of five rounds, pull the bolt back as far as it would go then push it back into place whilst also pushing the bolt working lever downward. The safety catch was then released and you were ready to fire. All you did to fire another round was simply repeat the procedure five or ten times (depending on how many rounds the gunnery instructor felt inclined to give you) until the weapon was empty or clear.

Just as luck would have it I was lying right next to the

dumbest guy in our regiment. His name (for the protection of his innocence in being a fuckwit) was Gunner Terry George and he was without doubt the sloppiest and clumsiest individual I had ever met. He drank for England in his spare time, his good fortune being that he worked as a drayman at the local brewery and I'm sure that a lot of the local pubs could never have received their full order if good old Terry was delivering it! Naturally it was a chargeable offence to be caught or even suspected of drinking on duty, but he somehow seemed to escape the scrutiny of the gunnery sergeant's usual sharp eye. Terry wasn't a bad bloke but he did have a brain which was limited in certain respects, and apart from falling into an unconscious stupor after having consumed about thirteen pints of Guinness and barley wine mixed together. His only two other joys in life were the Territorial Army and hitting things or people for no particular reason and in any order he fancied as the mood took him.

Most of our guys kept well clear of him as, although he wasn't a nasty character by any stretch of the imagination, he was definitely a liability and how he ever got past the examination board for the TA none of us will ever know. But there he was, right next to me with a fully loaded rifle and we all knew something just had to happen and sure enough it did! A couple of seconds before the sergeant gave the order to open fire good old Terry's switched-off and confused brain told him to do something quite unique, and that was to scratch his arse with his left hand while his finger was still inside the trigger guard of his weapon and this led to the weapon firing its first round directly into the ground about five feet in front of us all and sending a shower of mud and dirt up in the air.

It didn't stop there as the daft twat panicked and somehow

managed, with lightning speed, to eject the spent cartridge case and put another round into the breech and before the horrified sergeant could give the order to cease fire (remember, he hadn't even yet given the order to open fire!), he had fired yet another round, this time down the range but towards his left side and very much lower than was comfortable for anyone's safety. I still think he would have done it yet again if not for the sergeant coming up sharply behind him and taking the weapon out of his hands and making it safe. Most of the rest of the squad had cleared their weapons and had got up from their positions (as I was next to him I was the first one!) and moved backwards out of his way. Terry the Twat was relieved of his duties for the rest of the day and given a job cleaning the range rest rooms and toilets where he could hopefully do no more harm, a job which he was to be given on a regular basis after that incident. I think he was happier with a mop and bucket in his hands rather than a rifle. He was definitely a lot less danger to us too! We all had a good laugh about it, but how on earth anyone in their right mind would ever let a bloke like that near a pram let alone a fully loaded rifle is beyond me.

Another truly scary incident still stands out quite clearly in my mind to this day. The regiment was doing a live fire exercise on Dartmoor ranges. There were six guns, in this case the fabulous and totally reliable 4.2 mortars, and this was the sequence of events. The loader on the number two gun, unfortunately the one right next to me, had in its gun crew a very scruffy and useless dimwit I will call Pat Wells. I won't give you his real name because he's probably hiding somewhere on the moors still, walking around with a loincloth abusing passing sheep, muttering inanely and drooling profusely. Everything happened rather quickly and you know those moments where time seems to stand still?

Well, this was one of them.

The forward observation post had passed on the ranging coordinates to our gun emplacement, which were duly noted by the captain in charge of the battery. He in turn passed those instructions on to the gunnery sergeant in charge of the six guns that in turn passed them back to the bombardier or gun layer (that's the guy who aims it and gets to pull the firing lever!).

Once the gun is set to fire, the loader - in this particular case the hapless Pat Wells - picks up the mortar bomb, holds it over the top of the barrel (or stovepipe as it was more commonly known), and when the sergeant in charge of each specific gun shouts "fire", the theory is that he should drop the bomb down the stovepipe and duck sharply whilst holding his ears (they didn't have ear defenders in those days, just fingers or cotton wool). As the bomb is dropped down the stovepipe, theoretically the pin at the bottom of the bomb should hit the firing striker inside the barrel, ignite the charge and propel the bomb toward its intended target. Now there is a requirement of common sense which should tell you that you should always put the bomb in the stovepipe fins first, but our dear friend Pat had his own ideas and proceeded to try to insert it the wrong way round. This is not a good idea as there are quite a few tons of high explosive laying around the six guns, that could have blown us all to smithereens and I would not be here to tell you the story.

As luck would have it, even the TA has common sense built-in safeguards and the chain of command is thus. As the coordinates are given there are usually minute adjustments at the last moment. In this particular instance it went like this: down one, down safety, and of course the last command would have been the word "fire"! As the words "down safety" were given, the sharp-eyed sergeant in charge of number two gun noticed that was something clearly wrong and just before the word 'fire' was given, in one swift action grabbed the useless individual and the bomb, screamed the immortal words 'that man!' took the bomb away from him and placed it back safely on the ground. Within seconds the hapless Gunner was marched away and put under arrest.

Well I ask you? Who would have thought that anybody could be so dumb as to not know which end of a mortar bomb was which? We didn't see the prat again and we were all so relieved that none of us had the inclination to ask where he was. Dartmoor's gain was our lucky loss, so my sympathy goes out to the sheep and anybody who gets in that silly bugger's way!

The other strange experience that comes to mind was when I thought I had died and arrived at the pearly gates. It was like this. We had been on a night operation and the battery had been stood down for a short while and I had been relieved of my Bren gun for a couple of hours so that I could snatch an hour's sleep before resuming my post. As the other gunner took over my weapon and position I found what I thought was a reasonably comfortable spot to get my head down. It was pitch black, cold and misty and I was dressed in full cold weather clothing and I had my kit bag on which to rest my weary head. Within seconds almost, I was asleep. The next thing I remember was waking up (or I thought I was waking up) and stretching out and standing up. Only one problem, everything was bright, freezing cold and completely white. I couldn't see a bloody thing. I stumbled about, feeling my way in front of me and nothing happened. It was just like being in a silent white cocoon and I was petrified.

I felt around for what I thought must be the ground in front of me with my boots. I felt frozen not only with fear but with cold. My boots started to scrape on something and it felt soft and squishy, although I couldn't be sure, but still I persevered trying to make head or tail of my surroundings. I was by now absolutely terrified and had started to think I had died or something and this was where you ended up when you were dead! Suddenly I felt some purchase underneath the soles of my army issue boots and I felt myself starting to rise upwards. This is it, I thought. I'm being taken up to the pearly gates. This is what it's like. I felt such a prat when, as I got higher, I realized that I was climbing out of a shell crater (the one that I'd fallen so comfortably asleep in an hour earlier).

What had actually happened was that the dawn had broken and the very thick frost and ground mist had completely covered the crater I had been sleeping in and as the bottom part of the hole was all mud and I was so tired I hadn't given a stuff where I was just as long as I got a bit of kip! My head and shoulders were now above the mist and I could see the tops of the big guns lying still and silent from the previous night shooting. I nearly crapped myself when a quiet voice whispered in my ear: 'Bet you thought you were fucking dead, didn't you, Aby? Come on, mate. We've got a brew going and we're being stood to again in half an hour so get some scoff down you before we have to move.'

I went over to retrieve my weapon from my relief gunner and said: 'How long was I asleep for?' It felt like hours.

'Only about an hour,' he said. 'I knew that you'd wake up and crap yourself so we just let you have a lay in for a giggle!'

'Thanks.' I said, not letting on how near they were to the truth of the matter.

'Yeah,' said another of my gun crew, 'and you were humming and singing in your sleep, mate. That was a good laugh too!' Bastards! Good mates, though. What jolly japes we did get up to. So glad I never went to war. I think we would have lost with the way we carried on. Certainly if there had been one we would have given the enemy a massive advantage!

During my time (albeit short) in the Royal Artillery, I still managed to keep playing with the Hustlers and did an average of three or four gigs a month in between going on various courses up and down the UK, such as learning to lay (or aim and fire) a 25-pounder Howitzer or a large 5.5 field gun, learning to drive ten-ton trucks that towed the guns and limbers and operate a radio communications truck, become a motor cycle despatch rider (known as a Don R in those days) and was even sent on the parachute training course, as we were part of the Airborne Division of which my predecessor regiment 419 Heavy Artillery was attached to during the Second World War. My battery (which later was to become 201 battery Herts & Beds Yeomanry), the one I joined up with in 1959 had been in support of the Parachute Regiment and other units of the airborne forces at Arnhem and as recognition of that supporting role we wore the coveted insignia of the Airborne Forces on the bottom part our right battle dress sleeves, something I'm still very proud of.

I found out I would never have made a paratrooper as long as I had a hole up my bum as, although I didn't realise it at the time, I was shit scared of heights and aeroplanes. This fear was to manifest itself at a much later point in my life, which I will relate in a later chapter. Fortunately for me that more serious part of the training didn't materialise. I am still proud to have been a gunner though and mindful of the sacrifices that many of our old comrades gave in the line of duty. "Ubique Quo Fas Et Gloria Ducunt" is the Royal Artillery motto and it means: "Everywhere. Wither Right and Glory Lead". Good on yer, gunners everywhere!

Although it was a lot of fun doing all these things, the lure of music was far more appealing and within three years Brian and I handed our army kit back to the local quartermaster and were once again full time civilians without having fired a shot in anger. This was now 1962 and things in the world were changing, most especially in the world of music.

Chapter 15
All by Default!!

We still found time to play with the band, including a few USAF bases.

It just so happened that one night at one of these bases (Brize Norton, I think) we decided to change the band's name from the Jesters to the Hustlers. The reason was that the American Air Force had a new bomber in their arsenal at that time named the Hustler. We, of course, being young and naïve, had no idea what the word really meant! And so the Hustlers stuck. We continued playing the bases for quite some time until one fateful night. The lead guitar player, Brian Taylor, who had for quite some time taken an extreme dislike towards the singer, Pete, decided in his wisdom to throw his guitar on the stage and walk off. That left us with a bit of a dilemma, No lead guitarist!

Now, as luck would have it. I had been practising a bit of lead guitar (I'd managed to acquire a Fender Stratocaster around that time, much to the jealousy of Brian, who only had an old Burns Trisonic) and I fairly much knew at least half of the repertoire. The good thing was that as I could already play rhythm guitar it wasn't too hard for me to make the transition and play rhythm as well as pick out the lead lines, which in actual fact has stood me in good stead until this day. The next one to fall by the wayside was our singer, Pete. For quite some time he had been at loggerheads with his dad, the manager of the band. He had to be because he owned the PA, the van, the microphones and stands. So when he walked off the stage in a fit of temper that night in the middle of the set and refused to come back on, it just so happened that I'd been practising doing a little bit of singing as well. So guess who got that job too? Me!

Once again, we employed the old technique of playing the set about six times from back to front and from front to back. We had to play for nearly four hours a night, so it was really good training. And that's the story of how I ended up as a guitar player and singer - and every time by default. I was now getting at least £3.50 a night, which at the time was a lot of money. More importantly I was getting the experience that I needed for what was to come. The Hustlers got a new drummer in the form of a guy called Pete Luxton. He wasn't a particularly experienced drummer, but he certainly had some guts in his playing. For some reason or other the personnel changed quite frequently, so we became known as the New Hustlers, the Original Hustlers, the Former Hustlers and Hustlers Mark Two. And then back to the Hustlers again!

During this time we had built up quite a following, and we moved on to doing some more serious (or what I called serious) music in the form of Chuck Berry songs, some of the really early Elvis stuff and blues players such as Robert Johnson, B B King, Freddie King and Bo Diddley. Other players that captured my imagination were some of the great country players such as Chet Atkins. Still my greatest hero was Merle Travis and I'd started listening to some good jazz players too, among the greatest of which for me was Herb Ellis (who I was later on in my career to actually sit in with), Charlie Christian and early George Benson. I'd somehow always listened to jazz on the periphery of my love of boogie-woogie piano and blues in general, so I guess it was not an unnatural progression to listen to jazz as well.

What I would stress, however, is that although I am not a

natural jazz player in any sense of the word I am most definitely influenced by those styles. And strangely enough, it wasn't just the guitar I listened to; it was all the other instruments that turned me on to music as well. I loved a lot of the jazz sax players like Cannonball Adderley, Tubby Hayes, Don Rendell, Jerry Mulligan, John Coltrane, and pianists like Oscar Peterson, Thelonius Monk, Joe Zawinul and many others. Even at the heart of all of those different instruments I could still hear in my mind what the guitar should be doing, or maybe how the guitar would interpret it. I just loved the colour of all the instruments. I don't believe there is an instrument that I do not like. Just as long as it is played with heart and true passion, it's good for me and I feel that is an advantage because it keeps me focused on the depth of music as a whole.

Chapter 16
Moving Up and Onwards

I had now turned 21 years old and my mum and dad said to me: 'You have a choice, son. You can have a big party or a new guitar!' I chose the famous trademark cherry red Gibson SG Special and it was rare to see me without it. After all, you can have a party anytime, eh?

Around this time with the Hustlers and my acquisition of the Gibson SG I experienced one of the dreaded mishaps with electricity and power problems regularly suffered by musicians and bands in those days. We were playing at an old village hall in Eaton Bray, Bedfordshire, a Saturday night young farmers' dance gig. We had arrived early to set all our stuff up and the place was empty with the exception of ourselves and the caretaker, who was off to the pub the minute he had let us in. The drummer (Graham Hallwood) and the bass player (Dave Cakebread) were standing at the bar at the far end of the hall drinking a pint and I think Dave was smoking one of those Jazz Woodbine cigarettes! I had just tuned my guitar and it was plugged into a Burns Orbit transistor amplifier as I walked from the amp to the mike (a Reslo) just to position it in the right spot.

What happened next was frightening and quite exhilarating. The type of power source or current used in some of these old buildings was called AC/DC. It stands for Alternating and Direct Current. To say the least, it was dangerous to play around with and more especially if you had guitar, amps and PA systems plugged into it. As I grabbed the mike stand to move it the world went blue. I was thrown violently across the stage and I couldn't let go. It was as if someone had grabbed me, held me in a vice-like grip whilst shaking me and scrubbing my body with a wash board. Apparently the whole experience lasted for around thirty seconds or less, but in that short time in my travels across the length of the stage I managed to plough through Graham's drums (a £1,000 Trixon kit!) and nearly demolish them. I'd just reached Dave's bass guitar and amp (a Fender Precision and an Ampeg combo) and was about to trash them too when Dave realised that something was amiss. (He could tell by my screams and the blue crackling halo around my whole body!) He did the very brave deed of pulling the mains lead out by the wire and thank God the circuit was broken and I slumped gratefully like a sack of stones to the floor.

The guys helped me up and set everything back to normal and we all went into the dressing room where a bottle of scotch was produced and I was plied with a couple of very large measures.

'Thanks ' I said to Dave. 'I think you just saved my life.'

'Well,' he said. 'Me and Graham just thought you were playing around at first. Then we thought you'd started dancing and we then looked at each other and said: fat bastard doesn't usually dance does he? Then we saw the blue aura and that's when I pulled the plug out because I was worried about my gear!'

Great! 'Thanks lads,' I said and then noticed that something unusual had happened. Not unusual if you are sexually aroused, but certainly to my mind unusual if you had just been electrocuted and nearly died. I had the most magnificent erection a chap could ever hope to achieve (apparently a phenomenon which can occur when a male has just been executed!). So, here's my advice for the guys who are reading this little amusing tale. Forget Viagra and the like. If it's a solid woody you need. Just stick your fingers in a 13 amp electrical socket and wait. The results will either kill you or make you the proudest guy on the block! Please don't try this at home; I'm only joking. Really!

The Hustlers made quite a name for themselves by backing some of the visiting singers who travelled up and down the country playing the various town halls and theatres. It would usually fall to the resident band of the evening to support these artists as they nearly always travelled without their own backing musicians. We backed people like Vince Eager, who was known for his warbling tongue technique and the late, Dickey Pride, who had an incredible voice. He sang just like Little Richard, who is still my greatest vocal hero to this day. We also backed one of two of the more popular singers of the day, such as Mike Sarne (who had one major hit with a song called *Come Outside*) and Freddie Fingers Lee, a one-eyed mad piano player whose party trick was to take his glass eye out and drop it in some unsuspecting band member's pint of beer!

Our moment of glory came when we were asked to back an up-and-coming singer by the name of Neil Christian, who was a pure showman rock 'n' roll singer who had a minor hit with *That's Nice*. Chris Tidmarsh was his real name and he wasn't a bad guy really, but a real show-off and a ladies man in the extreme. The strange thing about his set was that it was identical to Screaming Lord Sutch's. And the drummer Carlo Little not only played with Chris, he doubled with David Sutch's band, the Savages. And as the set was identical we were able to deputy for Sutch's band on a couple of occasions. No problem there: the songs were identical, the band uniform was identical and the money was identical. Crap!

As a footnote here, I would mention that the guitar player

who I took over from in Neil Christian's band was none other than the legendary Jimmy Page of Led Zeppelin fame, who at a later point in my career we were to tour with. Just thought I'd put a bit of name dropping in for good measure! In fact, when David Sutch died (may he rest in peace), he shuffled off this mortal coil still owing me the grand sum of £15! Oh rock 'n roll - who'd be a band member?

As we now know, rock 'n roll's days were numbered and the general public had started getting into soul music. For me this was a great time as a lot of the music reflected how I really felt and how I wanted to play. You must remember that at this time I was still living at home with my mum and dad and the only time I'd been away was on courses with the Territorial Army. There suddenly came the call from Manchester. One or two of the guys that I'd played with previously need a guitar player urgently and so they asked me. I think at that point in time, half of the population of Luton's musicians had moved north to Manchester to seek their fame and fortune, so I fitted right in.

I enjoyed my time in Manchester. It was a very lively and down-to-earth place and I shared a house in a place called Moss Side, yet another big old Victorian house which had seen better days but provided cheap accommodation for students and musicians such as me. As you might imagine, there wasn't a lot of money about, and I think the average rent was around £10 per week, maybe even slightly less. But to be honest, we didn't care; we were just having fun playing music. Although we seemed mostly to play in the north we did occasionally venture south. And I seem to recall the ones we played at a place called Tiles Club in Oxford Street in London. Why travel to London from Manchester for just one gig? It was the kudos that took us there!

The Toggery Five were to all intents and purposes a

Manchester band and really stayed and played mainly in that part of the UK. We did play Scotland a few times, but we found it quite a violent place in those days, especially for bands. And I think because we had a singer in the form of Paul Young (a great guy) who was a ladies' man, the locals didn't care for us and tended to be more intent on beating the crap out of us, especially Paul, because their local women were not paying any attention to them!

We played a lot of good stuff in The Toggery at gigs like the Golden Torch in Tunstall, Stoke-on-Trent, and the Twisted Wheel in Manchester itself. There were some brilliant soul acts appearing there as part of their UK tours and we seemed to end up supporting a lot of them. We supported Rufus Thomas (*Walking The Dog*) at Stoke and I wasn't completely sure about him as, although I loved his music and still do, I got the feeling he didn't care much for white boys, or maybe he was just tired on the night that we played with him, but he wasn't very sociable and refused to share a dressing room with a bunch of local white boys like us. I might be wrong about him but there was only one dressing room and the only guy in our band that he would seem to have any time for was Arthur Hasford, our trumpet player, who just happened to be black!

He had a good laugh out of it, but we other poor buggers had to get changed and tuned up in the corridor! My playing was getting a bit more depth to it by this time and I had definitely started to acquire a certain feel to go along with all the soul tunes that we were now playing. It was steeped in exactly the right kind of mixture of blues/rock and soul for me and suited me down to the ground and I think this was really the point where I started to develop my own peculiar style if you like. I had started to dye my hair peroxide blond at this time as I thought it seemed a bit out of the ordinary and I was convinced it would help me in my quest to pleasure as many young gentlewomen as I could possibly get my grubby hands on!

However, that dream was shattered one dark winter evening in Warrington when we were playing at a club whose name I cannot remember, but will never forget the events that took place at it. The back entrance to the stage was over a long, high fire escape and our old ex-Civil Defence van that transported the band around was parked at the bottom of it. We had arrived at around six in the evening and set up our stuff and gone across the road to a greasy spoon café for a bit of grub. I think I had something like a meat pie and chips, but whatever it was didn't agree with my stomach and within an hour I was feeling terrible with stomach cramps and sickness.

We had to play three sets that night and I managed to get through the first hour without throwing up. I felt so ill though that I told the rest of the guys I was going to have to lie down somewhere until I felt better. They all said: 'That's OK, mate. Just go and grab a kip in the back of the van and we'll come and wake you five minutes before we are due to play the next set and then if you still feel rough you can go back again until we are ready to play the last set.' I was truly grateful for the respite and went down to the bottom of the long fire escape and climbed into the back of the van.

It was bloody freezing so I found an old blanket and curled up in it and dropped off to sleep. Now here's the good bit! I was suddenly and rudely awakened by someone manhandling me and saying such sweet things to me as: 'Come on, love, you'll be alright with me, give us a kiss!' It was some horrible, beer-smelling local drunk who thought his luck had suddenly changed for the better when he chanced upon my sleeping form in the back of the unlocked vehicle. He must have thought I was a blonde-haired female who had had too much to drink and was sleeping off the effects before rejoining the party upstairs in the club, because all he could have seen was my mop of bright blonde hair protruding out of the top of a blanket. He'd jumped in alongside me and started to touch me up too, the dirty minded git!

In those initial wakening moments I was just so groggy and still feeling wretchedly ill, I didn't have a clue what was happening. I came to that sudden realisation that things did not bode well for me and sprang fully awake. Not unnaturally I was incensed by this plonker's unwanted amorous advances, so now, as well as feeling ill, I was also feeling very angry and quite violently disposed toward him.

With hindsight I really don't know who was the most surprised out of the two of us, but I gave him an almighty shove and sent him careering through the now open back doors of the van. He picked himself up and looked at me with complete shock.

'Fucking hell, mate, I'm sorry,' he said. 'I didn't know you were a bloke!'

'What's that got to do with anything? I shouted back at him. 'Is that your usual method of trying it on with the local women, you brainless twat?' I'll give him full marks for trying as his reply was quite unbelievable.

'Well, you've got all that blonde hair, mate, so I thought you must be a bird! What are you then? A poof or something?'

Bloody cheek! As if it wasn't enough to be manhandled for no good reason other than this drunken moron fancied trying his luck with what he thought was an innocent sleeping female who wouldn't put up much of a struggle. He then tried to have a go at me as if it were my entire fault the cheeky bastard! I launched myself at him and tried very hard to land a good kick in his nether regions, but I was still wobbly from the effects of feeling ill and missed altogether, but instead I managed to kick a bin which was in between me and him. It hurt like hell and simply made matters worse.

He gathered what was left of his drunken wits and made a run for it as he knew I wasn't going to leave it there and it was a good job he did too. Just to add insult to injury, as he ran away he kept looking back and shouting: 'You dirty pervert! Bloody poofter!' and other nice encouraging lines! I slammed the doors of the van and made my way back upstairs to the club. Paul opened the door and said: 'Ay oop, Mick! I was just coming to get you. How are you feeling now?'

'Marvellous,' I said and just went back onstage and played. I didn't have the heart to tell the guys what had just transpired as I knew I would be in for a whole load of piss taking. Needless to say I didn't bother to go down to van to sleep again that night and just played the next set without further complaint. I did still feel ill but it was better to feel ill I decided than to get fondled and kissed by the local version of Warrington's Casanova! We live and learn. And I still had my SG to cuddle up to if I felt lonely.

I didn't bother telling the band anything until a few days later and of course they all said: 'You should have given us a shout we'd have come down and sorted the geezer out!' Yeah, really! The first thing I did when we got back to Manchester was to dye my hair dark brown; no more Marilyn Monroe looks for this boy!

Chapter 17
Deutschland over Alice

As happened with a lot of bands at that time we ended up going abroad and doing a residency in a place called the Party Club in Hanover, Germany. We played seven nights a week, five hours a night with the exception of Sunday, which was a day of rest, which meant we only played for four hours! It was, however, good grounding - what we called putting leather in the lungs. Again, I think the most money we ever got was around 10 pound a week. And as we generally ran up a tab every night for beer it wasn't long before the 10 pound ran out. Fortunately for us through, the nice ladies who frequented the club took a shine to us, which was cool because that meant we didn't have to pay for beer anymore. I immediately acquired a really nice looking girlfriend whose name was Alice, who attended to my every bodily need and paid my bar tab. But good old me being naïve as usual, I just happened to notice that most nights when we were playing, my new found girlfriend was constantly going in and out of the club.

One night after we had finished playing our last set we were sat around a table having a drink. I asked her: 'Why do you go in and out of the club while we are playing?'

'You don't know?' she said quizzically?'

'No,' I replied.

'You mean you don't know what I do?' she said with an even more astonished look. Until that point I'd never really thought about what she did at all apart from looking after me and paying my bar bill! (Isn't young love wonderful?) 'I work in the big building across the road,' she said, which of course I had noticed, but had not realised until she told me that it was legalised brothel.

'Aahh'! I said sheepishly (trying not to let her see that I was frantically scratching my knackers), 'so that's what you do.'

She smiled. 'You don't have to worry,' she said, 'we have regular checkups every day. The doctor comes to see us and gives us blood tests. So there's not much chance of you catching anything from me.' Which I suppose was fair enough, but I was more worried about catching something from somebody else that she might have caught it from! Let's face it; good nookie is good nookie and, although she was looking after the carnal needs of quite a few of the Deutsch male population, she was really in love with me. I know it's true because she told me so every night. I still had to keep telling her in moments of heightened passion that my name was Mick and not Fritz or Wolfgang! I think she just had a dull memory due to the strain of her job.

Anyway, I'm still here to tell the tale, and I continued to get free beer and nookie, so why worry? Halcyon days! Stints in Germany continued with another four months in yet another club, in Brunswick this time. Then on to Hamburg, Kiel, and finally back to Manchester and completely broke.

Chapter 18
Home Sweet Home?

Things did then become a little thin. This was around the year 1964 when it became so tight that we genuinely did not have enough money to even eat, let alone pay our rent. It was so bad that I remember all the guys going into the offices of Kennedy Street Artistes (or agents then) and almost begging for an advance on money that was rightfully owed to us, as the scumbag agent (again I won't name him but I'd bet he never starved!) did everything he possibly could to avoid paying us our due. After about an hour of us all sitting in his office and nagging him, he finally relented and gave us a tenner between us so that we could get something proper to eat. This was Friday and we had eaten hardly a thing except a few slices of mouldy toast since Tuesday because this rat bag wouldn't cough up.

Armed with that ten quid we made our way to a cheap greasy spoon café owned and run by a lovely Italian guy called Luigi in St Peters Square in the centre of Manchester and gorged ourselves silly on sausage, egg, chips and beans. We obviously ate it all too quickly and our stomachs just couldn't take the sudden intake of food, but it must have been great quality entertainment for the local office workers to see the Toggery Five Synchronised Projectile Vomiting Team performing their latest routine in the gutter outside the café, but not so good for Luigi's business. Dear old Luigi. He was a singer and performer back in Italy in his youth and understood the way things were for hard-working musicians and, bless his golden heart, he didn't kick up too much of a fuss, just told us to go around the back and got a few buckets of water and cleaned up. He was so kind that he said to us in his broken English: 'Whena you don ged a nothing to eat cos them no good bastardos a no give a you da money, just a come round and I make a sure you getta good feed!' Good job there are people like Luigi in this world. What would we do without kind hearted guys like him? I don't know if he is still around, but if you are, God bless you mate and all like you!

I thought I had cracked it when a few mornings later I visited the local music shop in Oxford Road in the centre of the city and was chatting to a mate called John Dickens. I was sitting on a stool playing a few licks with one of the guitars on sale in the shop. Just then the door opened and in came two members of Johnny Kidd and the Pirates. I must admit to being a bit star struck, as Johnny Kidd and his band were total heroes of mine and had been since way back when. I continued playing and after about ten minutes they both came over and introduced themselves. I didn't really need an introduction as I was all too aware of who they were. We chatted politely for a few more minutes and then I got a shock when they said: 'Mick, we've been listening to your playing and we reckon you'd fit into the Pirates perfectly and as it so happens our guitar player is leaving us next week. How would you feel about taking his place?' I was knocked out as, although the legendary Mick Green had left the Pirates for pastures new, it was still a very prestigious gig to have and one which I would revel in! Imagine going back to my home town and telling all my mates that I was now the lead guitar player for Johnny Kidd and the Pirates?

It was nearly too much for me to take on board, but my answer nonetheless; was a very enthusiastic 'Yes, I'd like that!'

I knew I wouldn't be treading on anyone's toes or letting anyone down as The Toggery had come towards the end of their shelf life and there were mumblings from all the guys about just how bad things were and that they were looking for new jobs or even giving it up altogether. Arthur Hasford had already left and Paul was talking about getting together with one of his old mates from the original band and forming a duo cum band called Young & Renshawe (they later became known as Sad Café) and I don't think we were included. So I made my way back to the band hovel in good old Moss Side and spoke to Clive about my bit of good fortune and, of course, Clive being the star that he is just said: 'Nice one, Aby. Go for it, mate. I probably won't stay for much longer anyway.'

So that was it. I'd made my mind up and I'd already arranged to meet the guys from the Pirates in the music shop on the following Monday morning to finalise arrangements, discuss the money etc. The main thing was that I'd got the gig. I was so excited it was unreal. I arrived at the shop at nine thirty. I wasn't due to meet the guys until around ten thirty, but I just wanted to be there first, I think to prove how keen I was. Five minutes later John Dickens came into the shop and gave me a real strange look. He knew what the score was and how much I was looking forward to this moment, but his face told me something entirely different. 'Bad news, Mick. Johnny Kidd was killed on Friday night in a terrible car crash and his bass player is in hospital with a broken back.'

I think I nearly fainted when he told me, not so much from thinking about the gig, but what a terrible loss the death of Johnny had made to me and thousands of others. I couldn't speak. I just got up and left the shop in tears. I was gutted about the whole thing. I'd only ever met Johnny twice when we supported them when we were youngsters with The Hustlers and he was very gracious, a great performer and to my mind a very nice guy. I don't think I was even bothered that much at the time about the implication of not now having one of the most prized gigs (to me anyway) or for that matter not now having a gig at all. The whole world felt like the colour black and even blacker.

I played around three more gigs with the last remnants of the Toggery Five and fortunately for me the very last gig I did with them was in London at The Tiles Club in Oxford Street, so at least I got a free ride back to Luton with all my kit. Although I really had enjoyed playing and living in Manchester and especially with the Toggery, things had come to the crunch and with a sinking heart for a whole host of reasons I wearily settled back down in the old homestead with Mum and Dad and enjoyed some good old-fashioned home cooking for a change.

Within a very short time I had acquired a full-time day job in the local cold store depot at the top of our road as I needed to earn some money and of course pay my folks a bit of rent. I was amazingly lucky with this turn of events and to say the job was money for old rope would be truly an understatement. The job was five days a week from eight o'clock in the morning to four o'clock in the afternoon and all we four guys ever did was to sit in a room, drinking tea and smoking fags and playing cards. On the odd occasion we were actually called to do some work, all we had to do was unload a lorry full of frozen lambs or other meat, stack it on a barrow, push it into the depths of the cold store and when we were finished, return to a nice warm room, our tea, fags and cards. The store itself was a huge rambling building left over from the Second World War in which they stacked mountains of butter. So much butter, in fact, it would have fed half of Africa! And as far as I know it is still there to this day! What an incredible waste. Naturally, I soon got bored with this job, but I put the situation to good use.

There were dozens of empty rooms in this building, and the boss there was a nice geezer and didn't really mind what we got up to as long as we were there to unload the trucks when they arrived, which fortunately for us was only about once a week. So I struck up an arrangement with him, as by this time I was working with a local band called Yenson's Trolls, which consisted of Andy Pyle on Bass, Clive Bunker on Drums, Jim Ledgerwood on keyboards and me. We were only doing local gigs really - that's about a 50 mile radius from home - but still we tended to get in a bit late in the evening , and as a consequence I didn't get much sleep. So the arrangement was I had a little camp bed which I set up in one of the empty rooms, and simply came straight from the gig to work. If there was any work to do one of the lads would come and wake me up and I would quickly put on my cold-weather gear, help unload the truck and go back to bed. The guv'nor was such a nice guy he even didn't mind that I brought my guitar and amplifier into work and practised during working hours as well as having a kip! Quite a cushy little arrangement and not only did I get paid for it but we occasionally nicked the odd leg of lamb to shove in the back of the van when no one was looking.

This arrangement lasted for about a year and that time Yenson's Trolls played at least a couple of gigs a week. For a very brief time I tried to put together a larger soul type band, but we only ever got to the rehearsal stage and I don't remember us ever playing a single gig. It was a lot of fun though. I'll try to remember the line up as best I can. It was Bernie Hetherington (baritone sax), Mick Chambers (tenor sax), Graham Waller (piano and insanity), Dave Cakebread (bass), Clive Bunker and me. All we ever did was play three times a week for about four weeks, get riotously pissed and smoked up, play a few good soul songs and blues tunes and have a great laugh. Really just a jam band with no direction or audience. Graham Waller kept us amused with his insane antics and quirky wit and I don't remember a time in any band that I laughed so much.

Nothing special happened really and the band more or less withered away. However, as a consequence of the total lack of gigs and general interest about the band, we disbanded amicably and formed another smaller unit with a couple of new members. Pete Fensome was and still is a bass player, but as we had already recruited a new bassist in the form of Andy Pyle, we fitted Pete in the band in the role of lead singer and occasional rhythm guitar player. We decided to call the band McGregor's Engine. The origin of this lies in my repertoire of silly voices and impressions. One of the many imaginary characters in my armoury was a chap called Mad McGregor, a train driver by profession and a drunken one to boot! McGregor was always driving his train toward anything that looked remotely like an Englishman, a wall, a mountain or a herd of cattle - anything he could destroy with his train as he was drunkenly but happily puffing away around the Clags of Claggy Maron (a remote mountain range that exists somewhere in the wild highlands of Scotland and my fertile imagination!) He would curse loudly all the while he was engaged in his murderous pastime, and the character became more vicious and wild, depending on how much drink I had had on each occasion Mr McGregor appeared!

Needless to say, I always had the guys in stitches with this imaginary loony and many a time when I went into his character I nearly trashed the van or the general surroundings wherever we were. A by-product of smoking hash, drinking beer and whatever, plus an extremely vivid imagination. I have to mention at this point that I was never really big time into either drugs or drink, but when funds were available, a few pints and a couple of spliffs were always more than welcome. I never went down the road of the heavy stuff such as speed, LSD, coke or heroin as I didn't like being out of control. I'd seen too many people ruin themselves and, on one occasion, kill themselves through the hard stuff. There but for the grace of God go I, as they say, but my indulgence was certainly not on a large scale, although I did have a lot of laughs when I was merry or mildly stoned. More later.

Chapter 19
The Reign of Mad McGregor

So McGregor's Engine we became. The band's make up and musical direction started to change drastically from that point on. We started doing much more soul and blues oriented numbers and the audiences started to warm to us more than ever. Unfortunately Pete wanted to do softer and more ballady kind of stuff, which most definitely didn't fit with the new vibe of the band as we had now become much grittier and harder hitting. So sadly Pete and the band parted company, but happily again on an amicable basis and we continued as a three piece with just me doing what I did best: lead and rhythm and vocals. This was around the time of the emergence of the harder-hitting blues-based bands such as the Yardbirds and John Mayall's Bluesbreakers with the astounding Eric Clapton. Jimi Hendrix had emerged as a major force to be reckoned with and this was truly an exciting time, most especially for me because this was the age of the guitar. I think this was where my life really changed for the better as now I felt that I had something to say. I think at that point, my whole attitude changed, I started ripping holes in my jeans, wearing garish shirts and even bought a pair of bright red boots. Up until then I'd been quite a conservative dresser really, suits and all that. My only concession to a bit a vanity and trying to look outlandish up until then had been the peroxide hair disaster - and I wasn't about to go down that road again for a while!

This suited me down to the ground, I can remember listening to every single blues record I ever bought until they were worn out. The band seemed to get tighter every time we played. We weren't really playing huge gigs, but I can remember one particular incident, which was extremely comical, when we played a place called the Luton Boys' Club. For some strange reason, there were two factions in this club: mods and rockers, but they always got on quite well and just enjoyed the music.

Now somebody - and I don't know who - started to bring cans of Crazy Foam to gigs. It wasn't me honestly, it really wasn't me, oh, ok fuck it, it was me! We had a roadie at the time called John Blackburn, a nice lad who would do absolutely anything you asked him and on this particular occasion we asked him to buy two dozen cans of Crazy Foam. While Clive Bunker was doing his drum solo, John made himself busy, by piling up every squirt of Crazy Foam he could on dozens of trays and as poor old Clive was at the very climax of his wonderful drum solo we covered him with every piece of crazy foam that we had. The effect was unbelievable: all you could see on the stage was a mountain of Crazy Foam with something that looked like a huge Brillo pad and a pair of arms with sticks, thrashing wildly from its midst! I don't think we'd ever laughed so much in all our lives. And you've got to give Clive full marks for being the consummate professional and not missing a beat. By the end of Clive's solo the stage was absolutely smothered with Crazy Foam, so much so that we could hardly stand up for slipping around in the stuff let alone stand up straight for laughing. We actually finished the number to a standing ovation and even managed to play two more before the end of the evening.

The organiser of the gig though was not best pleased and ordered us to clean the stage up before we left the venue. The rot, however, had set in. The next time we played there, guess what? Nearly everyone in the audience had brought with them a can of Crazy Foam. You can imagine the result. By the end of the night the whole place was plastered in Crazy Foam wall to wall. They even covered the promoter from head to foot in the stuff! Tee hee! Yes and you've guessed the next move too. We got banned! But what a laugh, so screw him, the miserable git. He was a smelly, oily individual anyway and needed a good clean.

Musically, we were definitely taking shape and I was in my element as this was the time I really got to do my stuff. Now don't get me wrong, I never subscribed to the old guitar hero show-off bit as some did, but I did enjoy having the freedom to stretch and enjoy myself and I know that a lot of good music was there waiting to happen. Things continued at a mild pace for a while, we did the rounds of small clubs and discos and I still had my daytime job (if you could call it that). I was getting fed and watered and had a roof over my head and Mum's cooking, so life was sweet. You know though, all of that is never quite enough and destiny was about to rear its head in the shape of the coming age of Tull!

Chapter 20
Tull Death Do Us Part

As I mentioned, we were playing plenty of discos and clubs. One discotheque we played was called the Beachcomber, situated not far from the place where I actually worked (although really, you could hardly call it work, given all the tricks I got up to). The discotheque itself was above a very popular nightclub called Caesar's Palace, conveniently situated in the back of a bowling alley. It was quite long and had a stage at either end of the room and a small dressing room in the middle. The music arrangements were very simple: one band started at one end and played for an hour and while that band were playing the last five minutes of their set, the other band would be setting up at the other end of the building ready to take over from them. I guess it must have been winter time as the place was freezing cold, and the band at the other end of the building were called the John Evan Smash. There were a six-piece soul band and they hailed from around Blackpool in the North West of England. The line-up of the band was Barry Barlow on drums, Glenn Cornick on bass, Neil Smith (nicknamed Chic Murray as he sounded like the famous Scottish comedian) on guitar, Tony Wilkinson on baritone sax, Neil Valentine on tenor sax, John Evan on Hammond organ and Ian Anderson on vocals, harmonica and flute.

They were pretty good as I remember, although nothing earth shattering. They did a good solid repertoire of soul numbers with a few jazzy bits thrown in for good measure, which I liked very much. Now here's where the weird stuff starts happening. When the John Evan Smash started playing McGregor's Engine trundled off into the dressing room. And that's when Andy Pyle dropped a bombshell on us, or rather, dropped it on me and Clive.

'I'm leaving the band,' said Andy.

'Oh,' we said, 'why is that?'

'Well I've got a job in Gibraltar, and me and the wife are leaving next week.' To say the least we were totally gobsmacked.

Andy was always the selfish member of every band I was in with him (I still rate him as one of the best bassists in the world though). It was quite clear that he didn't much give a rat's arse about what might happen to the band as we couldn't have got a replacement at such short notice. After giving us this wonderful piece of news, he disappeared in the direction of the bar. Clive went off somewhere on his own, presumably to cool off and ponder his fate. It was at that precise moment that Ian and Glenn magically appeared in the dressing room and I realised that they were having a quick breather whilst the drummer Barry was doing an improvised solo.

'We've been talking,' they said, 'and we really like your playing. As it happens, we have just been approached by a big London agency who deal mainly with soul/blues acts (they already had Ten Years After on their books) and they've heard us and said they would consider taking us on if we had a more blues/rock style guitar player that could sing too, so how about joining up with us? Our guitarist Neil is not keen on turning fully professional as he doesn't want to leave the comfort of Blackpool and his regular job as a Tax Inspector. We think with someone like you and your style of playing this will be our big chance. What do you think? We've got to go back onstage now, so have a mull over it and let us know and we'll exchange phone numbers before we part company tonight.'

Well, you could have knocked me down with a feather! What a turn up for the books. The next person to walk back in the room was dear old Clive, who by now had had a couple of pints and was a bit calmer. I immediately told him what had happened and being the good guy that he is and always will be, simply said: 'Go for it mate. We can't carry on without a bass player anyway, so we'll have to cancel the few gigs we've got left in the book for the next couple of months, so we might as well just call it a day for now. I'm sure that something will come along for me soon and I've still got my job at the car factory to fall back on until I'm really ready to turn full-time pro. It's a good break for you, mate, so take it while you can.' What a diamond geezer. No wonder we've been mates for nearly a lifetime. Things, however, were to change a little sooner than either of us expected and for the better too.

Chapter 21
The Big Move

This is where the whole thing started moving along at a fast pace all of its own.

After that conversation with Clive, I waited until the evening was finished and as everyone was packing up their gear went over to Ian and Glenn and simply said I would like to join the band and see how things worked out. They arranged a rehearsal in a broken-down old convent somewhere in St Helens, near their home town of Blackpool. The first couple of rehearsals sounded rough and ready but I knew that Ian and Glenn (maybe even John Evan too) felt that I was making a difference to the way the band sounded. The next decision was made by mainly Ian and Glenn, who felt that the best way to capitalise on the potential of better quality work and a faster route to success was to move to London and be in the glittering capital of music land. Yeah! Really! That wasn't much of a problem for me as I was living in Luton and had done most of my life, and London was only a half hour journey from there.

I just happened to mention that Luton might be a somewhat cheaper option then London and made a few enquiries into renting houses or flats in the area. Here's where the odd coincidences started to happen. The second place I enquired about for renting was a big old rambling Victorian house at the top of Studley Road in Luton. Number 2, to be precise. The very place where I had experienced my vivid memory of the "MMm tree", the flying bomb and my auntie crapping her drawers. By another amazing coincidence, it was exactly opposite the horrible private school called Woodlands where I was given what they laughingly called a private education by those two crazy old women all those years ago!

It seemed to me so weird that the whole house was available for immediate rental and ready to occupy AND the landlady didn't particularly care who it was rented to or what they did for a living. It was amazingly cheap rent, And to cap it all, the old Monkey Puzzle tree (the "MMm tree") was exactly where it had been when I first encountered it at the age of 18 months!

The fates were coming together in their strongest form for me and when I told the guys about it they were over the moon that they'd got something together so quickly. Now it has to be said that Ian and Glenn were without a doubt the most enthusiastic of the whole band and didn't seem to care much about where they lived as long as it was cheap, cheerful and had they had a roof over their heads. They simply wanted to be successful playing the music that they wanted to play, as did I. Well, within the week everyone had moved down to Luton and No 2, Studley Road, complete with its splendid "MMm tree" and had become their new residence. As I said, things had started moving really quickly for some of the John Evan Band … more quickly than for others.

Chapter 22
The Road Back Home for Some

I guess out of all of them I was the most fortunate one as I was still living at home with mum and dad. I had a regular job and an income. Studley Road was a five-minute walk from my house. I did have a car by this time, but it wasn't particularly reliable, an old Morris Minor Van full of rust and prone to starting problems so I tended not to use it very often unless I needed to transport gear or the blokes around to rehearsals or gigs.

So, within two weeks of the band moving to Luton the best part of the band left to go back home to their respective mums and dads, their respective jobs, hobbies and lifestyles. Tony the baritone sax player just did not like the South. Neil the tenor sax player left because he was a Jehovah's Witness and was concerned about the lifestyle he would have to endure and did not want to miss the regular meetings at his local Church. Barrie didn't give a reason. I just think he missed home and didn't like the house or the company much. We parted on good terms but we now had a new dilemma.

We had a quite a few gigs coming up to fulfil for the John Evan Band (John had decided to stay for the time being) and we had no drummer. I suggested that we ask Clive, as the guys had seen him play and liked his powerhouse style of drumming. I went straight round to his house that very night. His mum answered the door and gave me her usual quizzical look as if to say 'and what trouble do you want to get my son into now?' (She didn't like anyone that might have taken her dear little Clive away from his proper job at the car factory!).

'Is Clive about?' I asked. He came bounding down the stairs as he'd seen my old banger pull up outside and the guys clambering out of the back and knew this must be something important for us all to turn up mob handed. 'We need a drummer,' we said. 'Do you fancy having crack at it mate?' The look on his mum's face was priceless, bless her soul.

'Yes mate, I'd love too,' he said with total conviction. I guess that although the time span between McGregor's Engine breaking up and me joining the John Evan Band had been only three weeks he hadn't got a new gig and as he told me at later point he was bored out of his mind and would have joined a passing circus or travelling brothel just to get out of the monotony of his job.

Anyway, that was all settled and we got down to the task ahead of us, which was rehearsing and finally gigging. The rehearsals went okay and we did our first gig for the agency which had taken on the band. The agency was called The Ellis Wright Agency of Regent Street, London W1, later of course to become known as Chrysalis and the now Chrysalis Music and Record Empire or Dynasty or whatever. It was owned and run by the two by now famous and fabulously rich gentlemen called Chris Wright and Terry Ellis.

Chris Wright (or "Norman" as Ten Years After had nicknamed him) had already made strong inroads into the rock and blues scene with Ten Years After while Terry Ellis had as yet to make his mark with a massively successful act. As we all now know, that was to become the legend that is Jethro Tull.

Chapter 23
How Ian Became Ian

The band was really initially just a soul band with a rock /blues/ jazz influenced guitar player and didn't do any original material. We simply did covers of unusual stuff that a lot of the other up and coming blues acts didn't do. Ian started playing a bit more flute and that definitely gave an unusual edge to the band. We played most of the initial gigs under the guise of different names. (It was a ruse to just get back to the same venue I think!) There were such names as The John Evan Band, The John Evan Smash, The John Evan Blues/Soul Review and all sorts of crappy names. When we'd done about a dozen gigs under these pseudonyms John suddenly announced that he had had enough and promptly went back home too! So there we were once again in another dilemma. No John Evan and so we quickly had to rename the band and as Ian was the front man and singer at first we simply called the band The Ian Anderson Blues Band, then it started getting really silly with such daft names as Ian Anderson's Bag of Blues and even (don't ask why this one!) Ian Anderson's Bag of Nails!

It continued like this for a couple of months and during this time quite a few odd things happened. Ian decided to take a part time job in the local Savoy Cinema as an odd job man and cleaner just to supplement his meagre existence and pay the rent. All this time he was (as we all were, I think) starting to become weirder looking and acting. It just seemed to go with the territory, I guess. I think in his case it was either a very good act or he was genuinely going nuts.

It was a hilarious sight, as one day when going to meet him in the centre of the town in Luton, I saw him striding purposefully toward me dressed in a shabby old greatcoat about two sizes too big for him, wearing a scraggy and quite filthy beard, with a porcelain urinal tucked under one arm that he had nicked from somewhere in the storeroom of the cinema. Inside the bowl part of the urinal he had a paper bag containing his harmonicas and flute and I do believe some half-eaten sandwiches left over from his earlier lunch so that he didn't need to buy more food before leaving for the gig that night! Why he wanted the urinal to carry these things was beyond my understanding, but as I was not exactly dressed as a dedicated follower of fashion and had recently adopted the affectation of wearing two old-fashioned and rather large wind-up alarm clocks around my neck attached to a piece of rope, I really didn't have any room to criticise his motives or his dress sense!

Another memorable humorous moment involving Ian and me began when I had just met him after he had finished his morning shift at the cinema and he said that he needed to go to look at something he had seen in Woolworths. I followed him around the store for five minutes until he finally stopped at the lighting counter and frightened the lady shop assistant by trying on all the lampshades that he could find. The poor woman must have been convinced that he was off his trolley, but he was a band mate so I just stood still and complimented him on his various choices. He finally asked the mystified woman for a mirror to admire his potential choice of headwear. In all fairness I'm quite surprised she hadn't called some sort of security person to deal with these two seemingly insane customers by now. I couldn't believe it when she actually went to the next counter and got a hand mirror for him! He spent about five more minutes admiring himself in a variety of different lampshades before deciding that they didn't have a colour which suited the rest of his apparel! He very politely thanked her for her assistance and declared in a loud, theatrical voice: 'Come, my good fellow, we need to leave this fine establishment in search of rabbits!'

I wonder if that poor lady is still on this planet, bless her heart, as she certainly put up a good front even though she was clearly thinking that at any given moment, this loony tramp and his hairy assistant with the alarm clocks might have decided to turn ugly. Fair play to her, I say, and I still don't know how I kept a straight face throughout the whole incident, because when I got outside I just pissed myself. What a performance! If only there had been video cams in those days. What a treasure trove we would have had by now. That was Ian for you back in what I like to call the really good old days. Me being the old fashioned guy that I am still wishes there was a bit of that genuinely off-the-wall kind of thing going on with him, but I'm not holding my breath. He still has a great dry sense of humour which shows every now and then when we get together and I love those moments when they crop up.

Chapter 24
The Branding of Jethro Tull

As the first three months of the band passed, we started getting what could be considered quite a reasonable repertoire. We seemed to gel well together initially as a hard-hitting blues/rock outfit with definite leanings toward jazz, which stood us in good stead with a lot of the growing army of fans from the various clubs and pub venues that we were playing up and down the country. For some reason or other I started playing an instrumental version of a song called *Cat's Squirrel*, which up until that point in time I had only heard from Cream. I had been playing a slightly different version of it while I was still in McGregor's Engine, but it seemed to evolve and take on a life of its own. It was different nearly every gig but still just keeping the main unmistakeable pattern of the main riff. It was great to be able to improvise over the theme of the song and it went down a storm wherever we played. Ian's tour de force was of course that wonderful Roland Kirk song *Serenade to a Cuckoo*, which he played beautifully and with great passion and still does to this day when he is inclined. Clive even ended up with his own drum solo show stopper *Dharma for One*, which was written by Ian and Clive. It was manic every time and always brought the audience to its feet. Glenn was one of the most original and inventive bassists I've ever played with. His style was completely off the wall at times and naturally when he was in the mood to do a showcase solo he would have the crowd going wild too.

We were definitely "happening" as they used to say and we

were being noticed by such people as John Gee, then manager of the famous Marquee Club in Wardour Street, London. This was the deal. If John thought you were good enough to play at the Marquee, he would give you a chance by doing a support spot for the main act of the evening and your pay for the night was I seem to remember, around £15.00, which was deducted from the main act's money. They were usually on a percentage, so if we got a full house (and in 98% of cases we did) they were fine and everyone went home paid and happy. The support band though used to collect a following of fans as well as the people who paid to see the main band. This was always noticed by John Gee, who would in turn reward the support band with a top spot at some point to see if they would take off too.

It was about this time that Terry Ellis, our manager, had started doing some serious promoting and general wheeling and dealing behind the scenes to get the band to take off into the big time. To that effect he called a meeting in the offices of the Ellis Wright Agency in Regent Street and introduced us to one of the bookers, by the name of Dave Robinson, who had recently left university after having obtained a degree in history and, I believe, sociology. He took one look at Ian's trampish look (one which Ian worked at constantly to induce people to think he was totally off his truck!) and our general scruffiness and unkempt appearance and said; 'I have got a great name for you lot. Jethro Tull!'

'Who the heck is Jethro Tull?' I asked, completely puzzled but at the same time, thinking it most definitely was very original and had a certain ring to it. He explained that Jethro Tull was a real historical figure who had revolutionised the agricultural industry by inventing a thing called the seed drill using the workings of an old-fashioned bellow organ or harmonium.

The only seed drill I had ever known up until that point, I thought irreverently, was the one that I used in my pants and that didn't have anything to do with agriculture or harmoniums! He had a good point though; we certainly all looked like something that had been dragged across a dirty field or run over by a combine harvester. Ian especially fit that image, although it was never the intention for Ian to become known as Jethro Tull; it was just a name for the whole band. It was settled. Jethro Tull we would become. There was always some confusion with the fans as to the name. Was it the band? Or was it Ian and the band? But frankly it didn't matter to any of us at all and we carried on under that name and a right good decision it was too!

Chapter 25
Sunbury Festival 1968, the day we will always remember!

The band went from strength to strength; finally gaining the coveted top spot at the Marquee Club, which was actually a fortnightly or sometimes monthly residency depending on the band's other commitments. As I mentioned earlier, Terry was grafting hard behind the scenes to secure us some kind of recording contract and up until then he had not had a lot of success. I seem to remember there was some rumour about him going to his parents and borrowing some money from them and I've also been told that he simply got a bank to loan him the money with the aim of recording and producing our own record and then presumably punting it round the various record companies to see who would take a chance on this new and strange phenomenon called Jethro Tull.

We certainly had started getting a seriously good reputation, the audiences liked us and there were plenty of bums on seats considering the era, when most of the venues were not more than between 50 to maybe 120 capacity. Then, all of a sudden, out of the blue, it was our big break. We were booked to play the Sunday afternoon spot at the Eighth National Jazz & Blues Festival on 11th August 1968 at Kempton Park Racecourse, Sunbury. We took the stage at around 5.00 pm, just after Chicken Shack, and from the word go to the very last note, we couldn't put a foot wrong! I remember John Gee doing his majestic and very theatrical introduction of this new and innovative talent, direct from the Marquee Club (his words) and before he could finish introducing us, Ian walked onto the stage without his favourite tattered shopping bag full of harmonicas flute and sandwiches, as John had carried it onstage for him. Instead he was brandishing a large broom with which he proceeded to sweep John off the stage whilst shouting something like: 'Get off, you old poof!' and grabbed the bag from him!

Fortunately John had a great sense of humour and, ever the consummate showman, reacted accordingly and made a hasty exit stage left (or was it right?) with a mock look of horror on his face. The crowd went absolutely potty! What a start to a show. From the opening number (which I believe was *My Sunday Feeling*) to the very last number, the crowd cheered and gave us a standing ovation. If I remember rightly we also were about the only band at that time to get an encore and actually play it, as the guys that were organising the stage times weren't letting many bands do encores whether they were requested to do one or not.

That was it. We just knew that we had done something magnificent and that we were on our way up the ladder. Within a couple of days the news had got out that this raggedy-arsed band with the wild-eyed flute player who looked more akin to Wurzel Gummidge on speed than a rock band member had turned the Sunbury Festival on its head. The reviews were great, some even spectacular. Here are a couple of write-ups about the event to give an idea of what it felt like, written by some music critics unknown to me, so forgive me if I don't give a credit.

1. Jethro Tull was an unknown factor as at the time they had no album out. Fresh from a residency at the Marquee Club, I had read glowing reviews of their act from the MM and was most interested to see them. They blew us all away! At this

time a far more blues based outfit, they really had a huge asset in Ian Anderson, who it has to be said, was one of the most original and outrageous front men of the era. He of the rubber face, loopy one legged flute playing and strange body postures was completely to the fore in this breathtaking performance. This was a totally ON set as the guys flew wildly through their act with numbers like *My Sunday Feeling*, *Cat's Squirrel, Dharma for One*, and Roland Kirk's haunting flute based song, *Serenade to a Cuckoo*.

2. It was all fresh and exciting, bolstered by the excellent blues guitar of Mick Abrahams- later of Blodwyn Pig - and I was an instant Tull fan, an infatuation that lasted for a couple of albums and then waned somewhat as I discovered Anderson had ripped off the breathy flute playing style of the great blind sax player Roland Kirk. I must admit that I just got fed up with his facial expressions and as the material got more complex but less raw and bluesy.

However, at the time I loved them to distraction. Abrahams was in particular a real gem of a player, his fiery version of *Cat's Squirrel* left everyone breathless and begging for more. His slide work was exquisite and he really let rip on *Song For Jeffrey*. Anderson's vocals were of course most memorable, his flute playing gave a great jazzy and distinctive feel to the music and the rhythm section of Bunker and Cornick who were driving and inventive. A band at the peak of their powers, apparently this gig was instrumental in their gaining a recording contract, which would result in the debut album *This Was* in late 68.

Another quote from Glenn also highlights our feelings on that day:

'Sunbury was, of course, one of the biggest days in my life

as it was THE DAY when we knew we were going to make it. You cannot believe the feeling. I don't have many recollections about the festival other than our reception. I swear we were all in shock. I don't know if you remember the circumstances of our introduction. Ian used to have a nasty old carrier bag that he took onstage and in which he rummaged for harmonicas, his flute or whatever - all part of his image. John Gee walked onstage carrying the bag and the whole audience stood up and started cheering even though up until that point we hadn't even been announced. What people didn't realise is that we had been playing five or six nights a week in little 40 or 50 seater blues clubs all over the country and those people had come from all over to see us. The music writers were shocked because we had made ourselves famous without their help or without most of them even knowing us!'

Chapter 26
Fame and Fortune?

Within a week we were in Chelsea at a recording studio called Sound Techniques recording our first album. The recording engineer's name was Victor Gamm, which gave rise to a certain amount of piss taking from some of the more uncouth members of the band (okay, it was mostly me, but Clive had a go too!), but generally we just got down to playing the music and from memory most of it was done without much fuss and the general vibe from my perspective was good. I'd co-written a couple of things with Ian and he even let me have one of my own songs on the album, *Move On Alone*, which David Palmer did a very nice brass band arrangement for. Two things I feel I should mention here. The very first bit of recording Jethro Tull did was for the MGM label and it was a song that I had written called *Sunshine Day*. It was produced by a chap called Derek Lawrence who was very much in the mould of Micky Most and Joe Meek and suchlike. He wanted a guitar hero type record and seemed to think that this song suited the need. I went along with it only because to my mind it was our first recording break and no one else was interested at the time. Terry Ellis I think went along with it for much the same reason. They put the record out with a B side called *Aeroplane*, which had been recorded some months before by the original members of The John Evan Band. They even misspelt the name as Jethro Toe, making it a collector's item for years to come. Needless to say it didn't do anything of any great consequence and disappeared into the ether!

We were proud of our very first album though, or at least I certainly was. Ian and Terry (who were becoming closer by the day) decide to call the album *This Was*, as in Ian's words he felt it was simply a diary of something that was at the time and no more. I guess I didn't have the foresight and certainly not the business acumen to see what was around the corner, at least for me, so I just carried on doing what I did best, but by this time certain alarm bells were starting to sound faintly in my mind.

There were a few hang-ups for me, the first one being that, although I am certainly not work shy or lazy by any stretch of the imagination, I didn't want to be working eight days a week; it would have driven me crazy. Ian was totally opposite in his work ethic: he then and I believe still to this very day simply lives to work.

Now that's fine by me, but I am not cut from that same cloth. I like to have a bit of real breathing space and relaxation and my ethos is a simple one too. I love to work and will always get great satisfaction and joy from it, but I work to live, that's the basic difference between me and Ian. I don't begrudge Ian any of his extremely hard-earned money. He truly deserves every penny and I wish him every blessing and happiness that his way of doing things has brought him. He is without question a highly intelligent and talented musician and performer, but there have been moments when he was over the top with the serious bit. At times harshly unforgiving and to my way of thinking could be best described as a mood theme park! People often ask me about Ian and want me to even dish up some dirt on him (especially scumbag tabloid journalists) and the good news is that there isn't any dirt to dish up! My view and experience of him is just as I have described it.

Is he a mean person, Mick? I'm asked. He's not the most

generous person I know regarding money, I reply, but he is certainly one of the most honest people in the music business regarding the money that has been due to me from him directly. I'm asked if I like him and the answer is yes, I still love and respect the bonny lad despite whatever has happened in the past (the past is past!) or whatever he will happen in the future. It's just my view and my personal experience, nothing else. I would add that he is not entirely bereft of generosity of spirit as he proved by making a guest appearance on a solo album that I recorded in later years and he didn't charge me a penny or ask for any royalties. He has made many appearances with me and the Blods or the MA Band and again I've never been charged for that kindness. So he's not all that bad a lad is he?

One thing that is important to recognise is that, with age and experience, we all learn; and even mellow: and I think Ian has most definitely mellowed over the years and I am very happy that has happened as I truly enjoy playing with him and Tull every now and then because the music now between us has a really nice tension that is productive and heartening. Here is my point though, for what it's worth and anyone who wants to know. I consider myself to be a creative and highly motivated person too, but don't ask me to go down the same road! It would drive me nuts!

So I could see the cracks starting to form already, and it was truly a dilemma for me. The second problem was that I had grown to dislike Glenn and he made it fairly clear that he didn't care much for me as a bloke either, so there was constant friction and bickering between the two of us and it seemed that would never be resolved. Naturally, as he was Ian's mate from their home territory, I felt a bit isolated about certain issues and often felt kept out of the loop. Although Clive and I had been mates since we were almost kids I didn't particularly want to take any sides and that in a way made it even worse for me. Clive was then and is now and I know always will be just a lovely guy and a good mate and I think much like myself he just wanted to get on with the job. He didn't mind working every hour that God sent. We never fell out about any of these issues, we just agreed to differ, that's all.

I know to some people some of these points will sound trivial and petty but I was around 26 years old at the time and still (even though I'd hardened up physically) emotionally naïve. The last two hurdles for me were these. I was definitely being shut out of the writing and creative process and it seemed to me that every time I tried to offer something up to Ian to collaborate with, it was brushed over and the subject was quickly changed. I look back on that with the hindsight that Ian and Terry were completely right about the direction for Tull to take, as time has clearly proven. I really just wanted to continue in a similar vein to the one in which we had started as that was the one that gave me the most satisfaction. This once again caused friction between Ian, Terry and me. I just couldn't do what Ian and Terry wanted me to, either physically or mentally, and it came to a real head when the prospect of an American tour arose. I had realised that I really didn't like flying (oddly I loved helicopters and small planes but was terrified of airliners!) so this really did even more to unbalance my general train of thought. With all this crap whirling around inside my head and my troubled spirit, I started to rebel. Tull as an entity for me was no more. It had started out as what I thought was a cooperative effort, but it had now become to my mind more of a dictatorship spearheaded by Terry and Ian. Or Ian and Terry. Time would determine the outcome of that particular contest.

Chapter 27
The Curtain Falls on
Tull for Me

During all this time I had had a regular girlfriend called Stephanie, who had very big tits and a mum and dad who owned a pub. Well I ask you, what more could a guy ask for? Big tits, free grub and beer; what else was nearer to heaven?

For me this was true romance (I hadn't got it all worked out that well, you see). My mum and dad, being old fashioned, had always been of the mind that a young man should be married and settled down by the age of 25 and they thought a lot of Stephanie. So marriage was discussed in spite of my by now extremely wild looks, profession and behaviour. I know her parents were slightly apprehensive, but they nevertheless took me to their bosom as their prospective son-in-law.

So with all this turmoil going on around my musical career and my personal life, I was very confused to say the least. A decision clearly had to be made one way or the other. At a particularly unhappy gig somewhere in the Midlands one evening I just turned round to the guys and said, 'Look, I know this is not going to work any more with me in the band. I don't want to do the same things as you.' But I still wanted to "make it so to say". I did do one thing which didn't go down well with any of the guys (and I don't blame them for being pissed off with me either). I refused to go to a gig somewhere in the far North of England as I was really pissed off and tired of the whole crap game that was being played out between me Ian and Terry and, for different reasons,

Glenn too. I just got in my van and drove home, went to bed and stayed there. Pathetic, I know, but that's how I felt. Fed up, messed about, isolated and let down. This was an overreaction on my part, but there it was. I'm not going to apologise though because it was the only weapon in my armoury that I could think of to use as a tool of rebellion at the time. I've never felt very proud of that instance, but there you go. I don't have any regrets about the actions, just a sadness that I'd let an audience down and behaved unprofessionally.

I should mention here that at that time I was befriended by the late and truly great Alexis Korner, of whom I had been a great fan for along time. We got together one evening at his old flat and over a smoke and a glass of wine I poured out my heart to him. Alexis knew exactly what I was going through and he became like a second dad to me with sound advice and he gave it in such a kind, caring manner because he was a family man as well as being the true original blues man in the UK. He said to me: 'Mick, you've made the right decision because that band will go on to be something that you just don't want to be a part of and you'll never be happy by staying, as it will always be a pure dictatorship and nothing more. You've got more than enough heart to survive and overcome whatever may come, so go for it and do what you do best. Don't let anyone else tell you how to play; that's your originality and your talent. Keep and maintain it and you'll always know that you had the integrity to do so.'

I once asked Alexis to come up on to the Marquee stage and play the number *I Wonder Who* with us when we were headlining with Tull, but the request was quickly rejected by Ian and Terry and it pissed me off big time because he was my hero and mentor. Alexis passed on many years ago, but I have never missed a gig without playing that wonderful song

Me at the tender age of 15 months
a golden curly haired angel

On the beach at Walton on the
Naze aged 3 years 6 months, my
favourite place when I was a kid

Me aged 9 or 10 and the famous Piece o'
Wood Guitar. The very first one my Mum
& Dad bought me for the pricey sum
of £7.50 or something near. This is where
I started my Skiffle career

Tom Mix! Me and my colt 45!
Aged 6 in the back garden of
194 Dunstable Rd, Luton

Left: "Norfolk House" 194,
Dunstable Rd Luton. The
house I grew up in. I have
mixed memories about this
house as it was opposite the
school that I hated but also
held warm and fond
memories of christmas' and
the like.

Rght: Fred Abrahams.
My Dad in his youth I think
this was taken before he
married my Mum

Grace Abrahams (or Grace Chipperfield as she was then known) again just before marrying my Dad Fred Abrahams. She was the longest surviving member (so far) of the Abrahams family. She died on the 24th May 2007 at the age of 100 years

Left: Me aged 14 years after the Vauxhall Motors Judo team had just won some regional final. This was the part of my life that helped me fight back! I'm second from the right, bottom row

Me aged 11 years posing on our next door neighbours bike. It wasn't long before I got one myself!

Me in Hannover Germany with my Maryln Monroe hair colour. I soon changed it. There again Hmm?

PAUL YOUNG'S **TOGGERY**

The Toggery Five. This is the band I joined in Manchester. The lead singer was the late Paul Young who became famous in later years with "*Sad Café*" and "*Mike and the Mechanics*". This picture shows another rare glimpse of Graham Waller who normally hated being photographed and usually attacked the anyone taking his picture! Don't ask!

An extremely rare photo of what must have been one of Jethro Tull's first performances. I don't think we were yet called Jethro Tull. We might have been in the transitional stage of finishing off all the John Evan band gigs! We might have been called The Ian Anderson Blues Band or something similar. Take your pick! I think the pic was taken at a youth club somewhere in the North of England

Me at nearly 17 years proudly showing off my Fender Stratocaster. This pic was taken when I was the rythm guitarist for the first serious band I was ever in "The Hustlers" I didn't realise that although I was making the hire purchase payments every month, it was the manager (in this case singer's Dad!) who owned it and when the band folded he took it away! Story of my life!

A later Blodwyn Pig publicity shot. We had just done our first tour of the USA so note all the groovy clothes!

Right: An old publicity photo of "Johnny Kidd & the Pirates" one of my all time heroes. This pic was taken a few years before his sad and untimely death

A publicity picture for the first Jethro Tull album "This was" a very talented makeup artist from the BBC Drama department decided that as we all looked so ragged, it would be nice to make us look older! She actually said she based my makeup on Moses!

A personal photo taken during the late 70's of me and my lovely wife Kate. She's still putting up with me after 34 years bless her!

The second "*Mick* Abrahams Band". This line up to my mind, the best line up of the band at the time

The last incarnation of "*The Mick Abrahams Band*" with the late Wilgar Campbell on drums. This pic was taken by a fan in Italy Circa 1971-72 I think it was taken in Milan.

"*Wommet*" the first incarnation of what was later to become simply "*The Mick Abrahams Band*" Pete Fensome and John Darnborough left a couple of months after this picture was taken and frankly, I don't blame them either!

Me in more recent years, still giving it large, and happy to be doing so!

to his memory, *I Wonder Who.*

After I told them that I wanted to leave I made it abundantly clear that I would not just up and leave the band in the crap without a guitar player and told them that I would continue to do all the gigs as agreed (with the exception of America) until they had got a suitable replacement worked into the band. To me that seemed the right and honourable thing to do. I turned up for all the gigs as I agreed, but as you can imagine, the vibe was not a happy one and, from Ian and Glenn especially, almost hostile. I kept it together and I was putting a plan together in my mind as to where I was going next with all the new songs that I had been writing but not being allowed to use in the confines of Jethro Tull. I got a call from Terry Ellis' secretary who asked me to come into the office the next morning as Terry wanted to talk to me.

This is where it gets a bit surreal for me and I hope it answers once and for all the question. Did he jump? Or was he pushed? Terry summoned me into his fairly lush office and invited me to take a seat and simply said, 'Look, Mick, I'll come to the point. The boys and I have been talking and we've decided that we no longer want you in the band, so I'm afraid you're out!'

It took me a minute to take the look of incredulity off of my face before I said: 'What are you talking about Terry? I gave you notice that I am leaving the band and was I thought being reasonable and hopefully even helpful by offering to stay until you had a new guy worked into the band.'

'Well,' he said. 'That's the decision and it's been made' so that's that!' What a fucking total twat! I couldn't believe my ears. Here I was being told in so many words 'You don't leave this band, matey. We hire and fire and you're fired!'

I felt like tipping his desk on top of him and trashing his

poncy office into the bargain, but something held me back and I just got up, slammed the door with the resounding word 'CUNT!' And went back home to lick my wounds. What a load of bollocks! You can't leave, you can only be sacked. Unbelievable!

Chapter 28
Marriage and the Coming
of the Pig

It was just around December when I departed Jethro Tull. I had already decided to just continue in the direction that I felt I would have done if I had stayed with Tull or at least have been allowed to co-write stuff with Ian, (namely, blues and jazz-influenced rock music), so I cooled my heels for a week at home in Luton. I should mention that by this time I had made the decision to marry Stephanie and that was to take place around March the next year. I then called a couple of players from the old Manchester days, Jack Lancaster and Andy Pyle. And they were keen to put something together. We didn't have a drummer and so we auditioned a few and finally settled on a guy called Ron Berg, who fitted the bill perfectly. We didn't have a name for the band at that point and here's one for all the people who always ask the famous question, how did you get to be called Blodwyn Pig?

We were rehearsing in a small studio in Kings Street, Luton, one afternoon and whilst we were playing a familiar figure appeared in the doorway. It was an old mate of ours Graham Waller, a total nut job and great piano player from Luton and the old times in Manchester. Graham was a very educated chap with a degree in about everything apart from sanity!

He could always be relied on to come up with something zany at the drop of a hat. 'Just heard the new band from downstairs, chaps,' he said, 'and thought it sounded wonderful.'

'Graham,' we said, 'come on, man, you're good at this sort of stuff. Give us a name.'

He struck up a very theatrical pose and uttered these words: 'Thou shalt ever more be known as Blodwyn Pig! Toodle-oo, old chaps. Have fun!' And disappeared. We just stood there totally gobsmacked and peeing ourselves with laughter. What a name! What else could we call the band after that bombshell? So Blodwyn Pig it was and still is to this day.

Just one week's rehearsal saw us playing our debut gig to a packed house at the Cooks Ferry Inn at Edmonton. We got an unbelievable reception, and from that point on everything went swimmingly well for the band. Stacks of gigs were mounting up and the audiences were getting bigger every time. The band was going down a storm everywhere. By this time Chris Wright had taken over the role of manager. I still think that he resented the fact that Terry Ellis had one up on him by having a band break into the record charts with a number three album as up till this point he was still managing the very popular Ten Years After, but they didn't have a hit record until later in their career.

Within three months we were recording the first album, Ahead Rings Out, at Morgan Studios, Willesden, an eight-track studio, but still quite hi tech for the time. We had a lot of fun recording that album with lots of loony behaviour and silliness going on all the time, but in spite of all the good natured larking around, everyone worked hard together to create that original raw, bluesy, jazzy feel that I was looking for had I continued playing with Tull.

Chapter 29
Flying Pigs

The guy who produced both of the Blodwyn Pig albums was called Andy Johns, younger brother of the famous Glyn Johns, the Rolling Stones producer. Andy did a superb job in every respect and to this day I still consider him to be one of the best producers I have ever had the pleasure of working with. A little name check here also. The tape operator on Ahead Rings Out was none other than the youthful (at the time) Robin Black, who would later go on to produce some of Jethro Tull's work and at an even later point around 1996 produce another Blodwyn Pig album called Pig in the Middle. It was definitely happening for me and I was in my element around this time.

Just one of the comical highlights in the studio was when our drummer Ron Berg was asked to wear cans (otherwise known as headphones) to do an overdub. He was absolutely out of his brains on something or other at the time and genuinely didn't know what we were talking about, and found two coke tins and strapped them over his head with some gaffer tape, and walked around the studio with every one falling around laughing at him. Stupid boy!!

Around this time I had got married to Stephanie at Leighton Buzzard registry office and we celebrated our first night of wedded bliss in a poky bedsit that we had rented in Dulwich, South London. Not the most salubrious of homes, but it was only to be a temporary measure until I'd secured the imagined fortune that would eventually come my way through touring and making hit albums. What an imagination, eh?

That first Blodwyn Pig album, however, went to number three in the album charts in the UK. The audiences and venues had grown in the UK and Europe and a tour of the states was arranged to coincide with the album release there. It went eventually to number 50 in the US charts in Billboard and Cashbox (the two main serious record magazines at the time). It was at this point that I started to realise that I had a serious phobia about flying (I guess in retrospect a more irrational fear of crashing!). Naturally this made life difficult for travelling as I preferred to travel by bus, train or road whenever possible. I even wrote two songs later on for the first MA band album which can be heard on A Musical Evening with MA, which is about boat and bus journeys. They're called *Greyhound Bus* and *Big Queen*. I'll cover that in a later chapter, but now more about Blodwyn Pig.

We toured the US for three months quite successfully for a first attempt and the American people warmed to us. Our very first gig on US soil was in San Francisco at the world-renowned Fillmore West. We were opening for Country Joe MacDonald otherwise known as Country Joe and the Fish. You remember, don't you? Gimme an F, gimme a U, gimme a C, gimme a K! What's that spell? No, don't tell me, let me guess! Top of the bill was one of my favourite blues players, Albert King, and he was magnificent.

We worked from west to east, taking in a lot of major cities like Los Angeles, San Diego, Phoenix, Chicago, Detroit, Minneapolis, Minnesota, and Boston. We finally ended up at the Fillmore East in New York City where we played with Johnny Winter before flying home to a cold winter in the UK. The one disappointing moment on that tour was when we opened for Chuck Berry (one of the greats and one of my heroes) in Los Angeles. His band was a bunch of local guys who as far as I could tell didn't even have time to rehearse with him before the show. He did this odd thing of just arriving at the gig (in this case the Whisky A Go-Go on Sunset Strip) and about five minutes before he was due to go onstage, took his guitar from its case, stood at the side of the stage and wouldn't budge before the promoter had counted out his money right there in front of him. Having then been assured of his pay for the night he handed it to his road manager/minder and went on stage with a big smile. Up until then I hadn't seen him smile at all.

There was something very strange and almost false to his behaviour to my way of thinking, but I'd heard stories that back in the past he had been ripped off by various crooked promoters and so that was the way he did things and I guess I couldn't blame him for that. He was Chuck Berry and if they didn't like it they could lump it! One of the guys in his backing band told me that they were supposed to know every single number that Chuck had ever written or played and if they didn't get any of the songs right or at least to his liking he would fine them pro rata per song. According to this guy the band were getting around five hundred dollars for the privilege of playing with him more or less and he had this horrible habit of doing songs in entirely different keys to the ones they were supposed to be in.

It usually meant that the band would end up getting a heck of a lot less than they were due and in some cases they ended up with nothing. It seems that it was just the fact that Chuck Berry could play them anyway he wanted because he was Chuck Berry. I'm not quoting this as the 100% gospel but I heard this tale of woe from plenty of guys who backed him up here and in the USA so it gets you thinking. Anyway, he is still one of the leading influences on generations of guitar players, a great rock'n'roll poet and hero of mine. However, he gave me and the rest of the Blods the cold shoulder treatment that night and on another two occasions that I have played on the same bill with him. It would probably lessen the blow a little if he would tune his bloody guitar up and at least play like the Chuck Berry we all love. As you can tell, I was not that enamoured with his attitude then and even less so these days. There again, I'm not as famous as he is and I have to doff my hat to him still!

Sometime during the middle of this first tour, we played in Phoenix, Arizona, and as we had around three days off before going on to the next gig we all just lazed about, doing a little bit of practising and writing new stuff in our bedrooms. When we got bored with that we would just smoke a few joints and have a couple of beers. Nothing really heavy, but just generally relaxing. It was rare that we didn't have a gig on Saturday night, but as it happened there was a cock-up with some local promoter (or that was the story I was told) and as a result we weren't working. It was really hot and dry in Arizona even in autumn and the first part of the day was spent sitting by (or mostly in) the swimming pool at the good old Holiday Inn where we were staying.

One of the organisers on the entertainment committee of the local university had befriended us and had been to the first gig. I didn't think much about it at the time, but there was a motive behind his friendliness. Nothing sinister, but still a motive. As we weren't playing that afternoon, how about us giving the local university students a freebie and impromptu concert? Yeah, why not? We all said; 'Let's do it. It'll be fun.' What I didn't know was that about half an hour before the guy asked us to play dear old Jack had taken a large tab of acid and was starting to show signs of strange behaviour to put it mildly!

Acid and any chemical drugs were something which I

avoided like the plague as I had seen some of the tricks people got up to after having taken the stuff and it wasn't always pleasant. In this instance though it was not only disastrous, but hilariously funny too. Within half an hour we were doing a sound check (if you could have called it that) at the university main refectory and the word had spread of the impending free Blodwyn Pig concert. Students had started to jam their way into the hall and within a short while it was full to capacity. An air of anticipation fell over the waiting audience as we took to the stage. That's when it all went south!

The PA system was not particularly good, but we could have got by, I guess. The main problem was that Jack was now into a full blown mega trip and totally off his nut. He was actually dribbling at one point, I'd swear to it! For those Blod fans who remember us in those wild days, you will know that Jack, being the very talented multi-instrumentalist that he is, used to play two saxophones simultaneously (and at the same time too!) for the opening number which in this case was *It's Only Love*. With his dextrous ability, this was usually no problem for Jack, but as he was stoned out of his head it made a considerable difference in this instance.

We had acquired some pretty groovy clothing (or at least we thought it was) during that first visit to the USA and all of us were wearing suede or leather trousers, colourful tie-dyed hippie-type shirts and the obligatory belts and hand tooled bags. Jack was no exception and had spent a fair few dollars on his own personal wardrobe of which his pride and joy was a beautiful heavily hand-tooled leather Navajo Indian bag encrusted with native Indian symbols and blue jewellery. He had this work of art constantly hanging around his shoulder. He also had hanging from his person a whole host of the various instruments that he would be using throughout the

111

set. These were hung on straps and various attachments so they could be brought quickly to bear as and when he needed them. There was first of all his main instrument, the tenor sax, a bent-out-of-shape soprano saxophone (nicknamed "the phoon horn"), an alto sax and lastly his flute.

Poor geezer was so bewildered that when I counted 'One, two...one two three four' to bring the song in, instead of putting the saxes in his mouth, he actually stuffed his bag in there instead! I could hardly sing for laughing and the rest of the guys nearly fell over at the odd sight. Still Jack persevered for a few seconds trying to get a tune out of his bag and just looked confused as to why nothing was working. The audience thought it was a part of the act I suspect, as they all started pissing themselves laughing too and they clapped really loudly at this new show of ours. Jack was now in a total state of meltdown. He clearly couldn't fathom out what had happened and tried desperately to find the right combination of instruments with which to join in the number. What made me laugh most of all was that when he actually realised it was his bag that he was trying to play and not his saxes he pushed it away from his mouth as if he just swallowed a red hot potato and shouted 'Aarrgghh!!' The poor lad was in a state of total confusion, but I've got to give him extra points on this one as he just kept grinning all the way through it as though nothing was out of the ordinary. I don't remember him being together with the band on any of the numbers in the musical sense of the word, but he was very happy. The audience got a free gig and a bit of a cabaret show so they were happy and we all had a great afternoon's entertainment, but musical it wasn't!

Chapter 30
The Pig Goes On

We started back in earnest after Christmas and I think we were trying very hard to impress folk with our recently acquired USA clothing such as leather and, in my case, a beautiful pair of blue suede trousers with frills, native Indian jewellery, brightly coloured tie-dyed shirts and the ever growing length of our hair!

I must confess to having acquired a bit of an "attitude" for a short while, which wasn't particularly unpleasant or anything but I certainly remember acting a bit snotty and a bit above my station every now and then when something pissed me off or wasn't quite how I felt it should be. Thank God I took a reality check, kicked myself squarely in the arse, dispensed with that affectation and treated it as an experience gained and quickly lost! In layman's terms it's called behaving like a bit of a dickhead. Enough said!

We were even more successful in the UK and Europe. We played quite a few festivals, including the very first Isle of Wight rock festival and went down a storm. We were with our old chums Jimmy Page and John Bonham and we always felt comfortable around Led Zeppelin. They were and still are one of the greatest rock bands on planet earth (along with The Who).

I remember arriving home at five minutes to nine on that day and sitting down in front of the telly just in time to see ourselves performing and getting a major amount of coverage on the ITN nine o'clock news.

It was then time to get down to recording the second

Blodwyn Pig album, *Getting to This*, at Olympic Studios at Barnes Bridge near Hammersmith, with some overdub work at Trident Studios in Wardour Street, London.

The songs on this album had a different energy and feel and, of course, we now had the additional luxury of 16 tracks to record with. We took full advantage of the new technology and used it to layer guitars and saxes to get a generally thicker sound. Once again, young Andy Johns was in the producer's chair and he did yet another great job. I still recall it as an all round happy session but there were a couple of incidents that I can now reveal the truth about.

Number one fact. Yes, I did sing a verse of *Variations On Nainos* with my head in a bucket of water with a mike positioned over it! Well, I was stoned out of my mind at the time and the guys bet I couldn't do it without passing out. Jack couldn't believe his ear and eyes, and being the playful bugger he is, said with a very serious look on his face, 'Well, that's all very well, but I bet you a tenner you couldn't double track it!' I proved them all wrong: I even double tracked it with the same bucket. It's the truth. There weren't such things as voice changers in those days, so I just improvised as best I knew how! Eat poo and choke, Lancaster! He still hasn't coughed up the money to this day. For the many people who have asked me over the years, why the title *Variations On Nainos*? It's me taking the piss out of Ian Anderson's name. 'Nainos' is of course 'Son Ian' backwards and 'Variations' was about the way his moods varied from day to day. Well he took the piss out of me with the song *Don't Wanna be a Fat Man*, so it was my little (not nasty but humorous) dig back at him. Alright Ian, my old son?

Chapter 31
Swine Behaving Badly

There was another hilarious event at the Chrysalis offices at about the same time. I had been called into the office of Doug Darcy on my way to the studios one morning and met up with the infamous John Bonham, one of the world's greatest rock drummers ever to hold a pair of sticks and legendary member of Led Zeppelin (who we had a great time touring with here and in Europe) and also a good drinking buddy. All of a sudden Stan Webb from Chicken Shack appeared. (He was the only guy I know who had his own personal toilet wherever he went. He simply stood at the bar, lobbed his old chap out and pissed up against the bar. It saved time he used to say!)

'What about a drink or fifteen?' said Bonzo with a grin.

'Why not?' we all agreed, made our way to the nearest pub and proceeded to get riotously pissed (it was them that made me do it. I didn't want to really! Yeah, really!). We were totally steamed by the time we got back to the offices and we were in a playful frame of mind to say the least.

'Here lads, let's have a bit of fun,' said Stan with a devilish look on his face.

Poor old Doug Darcy, the office poser number two, has never been the same since three drunken hooligan musos burst into his office armed with rolls of gaffer tape and proceeded to mummify him from the neck to his feet. His screaming protests were to no avail. The unfortunate agency manager was then frog marched to the lift and sent up and down five floors a few times to see what the effect would be.

As if that was not enough fun, we then hit upon the brilliant plan of taking him to the roundabout in Oxford Circus and leaving him there whilst watching from a safe distance across the road from a local boozer. He hopped around asking passers by to help him, but to no avail. Most people thought he was an idiot escapologist who had just simply cocked his act up. We did however have the decency to tell Nick Blackburn, Chrysalis's main accountant and office poser number one, of his whereabouts and someone was dispatched to free him.

(I spoke with him a while back at the 30th anniversary of Chrysalis party at which I was a guest. Chris Wright had asked me along and asked me to play with the house band, which I did, alongside some of the good old lads from the Chrysalis Music stable: Leo Sayer, Gary Brooker from Procul Harum and Midge Ure. The minute we met, Doug referred instantly to this incident, which up until that point I had thought had put me at the very top of his shit list, but instead of calling me all the names in creation, he congratulated me for having given him a wealth of anecdotes at after dinner speeches! I should have charged him commission.)

We then concentrated our combined drunken efforts on destroying the office of Bill Harry, the likeable Chrysalis publicist, by piling up all his furniture in the middle of the room and hanging his typewriters out of the window attached to a piece of rope. As he was always pissed (this particular day being no exception) he didn't seem to notice. To complete a good day's work we finished off by changing all the name plates on the doors and peeing in most of the metal waste paper bins. I don't remember much more about the rest of the day except to say I didn't make it to the studio. Fortunately Jack was just doing overdubs that day so I wasn't needed for any work, which was just as well.

Chapter 32
Getting To This

Back in the studio the next day, (and sober, just) the work continued at a good pace until arguments started to break out about who got credits for which song and other petty stuff, which was stupid and really boring. So to keep everybody happy I gave Andy Pyle (Andy was always whingeing about getting something of his on the album) a song of his own, Worry, although in truth he just came up with the riff for the song and I arranged and did the words for it.

To further the peace I also gave Ron Berg a credit for *Summer Day*, although his only musical contribution apart from drumming was a massive sneeze at the end of the song. The mind boggles! Jack, however, gave a great musical contribution to the album as a whole, *San Francisco Sketches* being the most notable, and we never fell out over song writing credits or other crap like that. The album got finished in good time and everyone was pleased with the result. Sadly for me though, the rot had started to set in with all the petty squabbles and ego problems, but as I was always one for an easy life I let it ride and continued as best I knew how. The album was released and went to number three in the album charts once again, remaining between three and five for some time.

On a very happy note, I remember one evening when Charlie Watts was in the studio doing something or other, he popped his head around the corner of the editing room and said, 'That sounds really cool. Mind if I sit down and have a listen?'

'No problem, mate,' we said. We'd been big fans of the Stones for years, but up until that point had never met any of them, so this unlikely encounter was a real treat for me and after chatting with Charlie for a while about Alexis Korner and a few people we both knew and had some common ground with, I went away with the lasting impression that he is a truly down-to-earth, nice guy. On the very same day I bumped into George Harrison on the way out of the studio and was shocked to discover that he not only knew who I was but that he liked a lot of the stuff that Blodwyn Pig had done. Again, after chatting with him for a short time I got that feeling that he, unlike some of the rich and famous celebrities that I've met in my time, was one of the real genuine nice guys. Believe me when I tell you that meeting up with people whose work you like and respect and finding out they're also decent people is a real bonus. It's a privilege to have come in contact with them.

Just before the second album, *Getting to This*, was released we did a tour of the UK with Ten Years After, which as I recall was a sell-out, and to my mind was the best tour we'd done yet. A remarkable and absolutely true incident from the period still sticks out in my mind, when we played Newcastle City Hall. It was a storming gig and at the end of the set I got mobbed by a crowd of fans. The sentiment was wonderful, but in that mob of fans, there wasn't one female! Not bloody one! I wasn't ungrateful for the sudden adulation, but I ask you. Oh well, I didn't set out to become a sex symbol, so I wasn't that disappointed.

Chapter 33
Vandals of a Higher Class

Directly after that gig, we drove down to Oxford to do a spot at the Oxford Keeble College "Yak" Ball (don't ask!), which was a very poncy do with all the newly qualified student lawyers and future bankers (yes I did say bankers!) having paid around £100 a ticket, dressed in expensive finery and acting like they already owned the best part of the country. I hated being there from the word go, but a gig is a gig, so I just resigned myself to a rather dull rest of the day (it was by now 3 o'clock in the morning).

We were shown into a beautiful oak-panelled room that contained some period furniture, lots of bookshelves and other fine things. In the middle of the room a small trestle table had been set up with a paper table cloth, A jug of beer, a few cups, some mouldy, ancient-looking sandwiches and some fancy cakes. The geezer who showed us into the room then informed us that this was to be our dressing room for the next three hours as we were not required to play until 6am! He also then told us in one of those awful condescending, jolly hockey sticks-type voice that we were not allowed out of the dressing room area (except presumably for calls of nature) and certainly not allowed to mix with the guests. What a total twat! That was like a red rag to a bull as far as we were concerned. We were tired, hungry and pissed off, having already driven to Newcastle - 226 miles - played a gig, and then driven another 260 miles back to Oxford (thanks to the terrific knowledge of UK geography displayed by the Chrysalis agency) to be confronted by this chinless hooray Henry who clearly didn't like commoners on his patch and thought he was doing us some kind of big favour.

Within five minutes of his departure we sent Ron out to forage for booze and whatever else he could find to relieve the tension and boredom. We told him he would be best suited for the task as he was clearly the cleverest at this sort of thing and the dopey prat believed us! Sure enough, 10 minutes later good old Ronnie boy came back with five magnums of champagne that he'd nicked from some legless students' table (he actually told them that it was okay for him to take them as he was in the band, so they just let him swipe them!) and we proceeded to get totally "rat-arsed". You know those wonderful silly moments when someone starts flicking little crumbs of food at each other, well that's just what did happen, just total silliness and up until that point, quite harmless fun. Everyone was just making a load of noise and falling about laughing, when all of a sudden there was this hammering on the door.

We thought it was Chinless Henry coming to bollock us for making a row. Someone shouted: 'Come in then', and I remember Jack actually standing with his head inside the lamp standard and the rest of us standing in freeze-frame mode, pretending we didn't exist. I opened the door and there stood a dishevelled geezer, obviously pissed out of his mind, bow tie awry, his glasses half broken and bits of vomit staining his tuxedo.

'Yes,' I said, 'what can we do for you?'

'What are you chaps doing in here?' he asked in a slurred voice.

'Nothing really mate,' said Ron, 'just smashing the room up, that's all!'

'What a fucking great idea,' said the little drunken toff (he was about five feet tall). 'Can I help?'

'Help yourself, mate,' we all said, pissing ourselves laughing. Now this is where things really took off as this guy came charging into the room and suddenly went into what can only be described as "helicopter attack mode". He stood in the middle of the room and started going round in circles trashing everything he touched. The table was the first casualty; that went over and splattered food and drink (if you could call it such!) everywhere. He then climbed onto the chaise longue, jumped up and down on it until it broke in three pieces, following it up with running along the bookcases and throwing all the books out of the window.

By this time we were all in hysterics as this nutter smashed nearly everything he could lay his hand to. 'Don't forget the lamp standard,' I encouraged him, and sure enough that went flying through the window too!

All the time that this was happening, our roadie John Peverett was rolling a very expensive-looking Oriental rug up, I thought to protect it from serious damage. I was wrong; he simply took advantage of the confusion to hump it outside and into the crew bus. 'My missus has always wanted one of these,' he said. Cheeky bastard!

The room now resembled a Beirut bombsite and our new-found friend and auto-destruction cabaret act was lying in the middle of the mess, shouting 'Yes! Yes! Yes! I've always wanted to do this.'

'Do what?' we asked.

'Trash this room,' he said.

'Why?'

'Because it's my room.' came the reply, 'and I'm leaving next week and I hate the place!' We eventually got ourselves together sufficiently to play and went on stage at around 6.30am to a crowd of 30 people nearly all of whom were either asleep or incapable of listening to anything. It was shite!

The next afternoon we called in at the office for some money and were summoned into Kenny Bell's office (head of Chrysalis agency and chief harbinger of all things joyful) who asked what the bloody hell we thought we were playing at, as he had received a call from the Keeble College entertainments' officer to complain that £500 worth of damage had been done to the room that we had occupied the previous evening, and we would be getting a bill for that amount. He just didn't believe a word that we told him and called us a bunch of irresponsible wankers, blah, blah, blah. Miserable git, never knew how near he had come to receiving the dreaded gaffer tape treatment that day. I knew I'd get a chance one day to set the record straight, so there it is. Let anyone deny it!

Chapter 34
High Altitude Problems

It was time for the second US tour and by now my acute phobia about airliners had got seriously worse. So much so that to avoid flying I left a week earlier than everyone else and took the QE2 to New York and the rest of the guys met me at the first gig which this time started in New York at the Fillmore East. We were opening for Chicago (who incidentally very nearly did a cover of *See My Way*) and Taj Mahal, who was magnificent.

I did take some internal flights and eventually flew home as there was no boat available. I must have taken so many tranquillizers on that tour just to get on the aeroplanes I was lucky to remember if I was awake most of the time.

We played The Boston Tea Party with Spirit and my old mate Robin Trower and that was a stunning gig. In the hotel room that night directly after we got back, Andy was suddenly finding it hard to breathe and had an anxiety attack (we didn't know what it was at the time as they hadn't invented a name for the condition yet). We thought he was dying so we called the emergency services and they sent two bored, scruffy overweight cops out to deal with the situation. It seemed that their only interest was to see if they could get some long-haired hippie-type freaks (that's obviously what they thought of us) for a minor drugs bust, but by the time they had got fed up with asking stupid and pointless questions Andy had started to feel better. It wasn't anything to do with drugs or drink, as that particular evening no one had even had so much as a spliff or a can of beer, so thanks for the help, guys, and thank God that most cops and emergency service workers that we met there were without a doubt some of the finest people whose acquaintance I have had the pleasure of making. Great, isn't it, how two dumb, lazy, fat, useless twats can spoil it for all the real good guys out there?

Chapter 35
Rednecks, Guns and Rock'n'roll

I remember that time in the States as a mixture of good music, good fun and some scary experiences thrown in for good measure. One such incident was with some good ol' redneck boys in Joplin, Missouri, who didn't care very much for our long hair or looks in general. We were staying in a fairly typical Holiday Inn-type hotel and got into a lift which contained a couple of seriously big, well-dressed but violent-looking characters. One turned to the other and proclaimed in a loud voice: 'It's a real shame that every time you see strange creatures that look like they ought to be shot, you ain't carrying a gun!' It's a shame also that they were unaware that I was a qualified marksman with a pistol as well as rifles and shotguns, as that happens to be one of the sports that I have enjoyed for over 40 years, although I have to say that I've never had the desire to shoot anyone just because they looked different and certainly not in the confines of a lift. It would hurt your ears something alarming, I can tell you!

As a by note; I've been around guns since my early years, have always been fascinated with them, took up shooting as a hobby and over the years have shot every conceivable type of weapon. I even shot with a police team and did a couple of practical and combat pistol courses, which was challenging but I seemed to get through okay with some good scores and it has always been very satisfying. I maybe should mention that as some of the people in the music industry are a bit "precious" about firearms, there have been one or two works of fiction made up about me for whatever purposes their authors may have had.

One in particular was when we played at The Nags Head in High Wycombe. Oddly enough, I've only read this work of art recently and it came from a promoter who is not a particularly pleasant chap who I know dislikes me - and the feeling is entirely mutual. He blatantly accused me of shooting all the lights out onstage at the club with an air pistol whilst the audience was in the club too! The truth was that I was playing around with a harmless plastic toy pellet gun whilst waiting for the sound guy to get things together and certainly didn't break anything, least of all while any members of the public were about. I'm not going to dignify his bullshit by naming him as he did me, but he knows who he is and, according to his own self made-up legendary status, he was one of the most influential people in the music industry. A legend in his own mind more like!

A true and amusing story about pellet guns relates to a dark and cold winter's night when Blodwyn Pig were playing at Plymouth. I think it must have been the Van Dyke Club as that was the main club gig around that area. The thing that sticks out in my mind was that we didn't have to go back to London as we were playing the next night somewhere in Wiltshire on the way back home. We couldn't afford swanky hotels in the UK as Chrysalis' expense account didn't run to that kind of extravagance. Our roadie Mick had found us cheap and nasty accommodation somewhere just outside Plymouth and also a bit off the beaten track. It was owned and run by a couple of rather strange-looking ladies who, upon setting eyes on us said all they had available was the dormitory at the top of the house. Beggars can't be choosers, we were all tired and so the dormitory it had to be: three floors up with little dim 25-watt bulbs to light the passages and stairs. We finally arrived at our designated dorm and it was like an old army billet, with eight iron-frame beds, woollen blankets, one pillow each and one bare light bulb near to the door. Not the Hilton and it was freezing cold too.

We sat around and shivered under our blankets and as there were a couple of joints floating about somewhere (Mick was our regular roll-up man) we started to get the giggles and acting daft generally. No problem there really and after a while we became quieter and settled down to a bit of kip. Only one small problem: no one wanted to get out of bed to switch the light off as it was colder than a polar bear's knackers!

'Come on,' Ron said. 'Put the light off.'

Now, being the mischievous rascal that I have always been, I said to Ron who as far as I could tell was the nearest to the switch: 'You're the nearest, so why don't you turn it out, you lazy git?'

More giggles ensued and Jack asked: 'Have you got that pellet gun in your bag, Mick?' As it happened I did. 'Well then,' said Jack, 'you put the light out. You're Billy the Kid or so you think!' What could I do? This was a challenge to my sharp shooting skills!

I pulled the gun out of my bag and with absolutely not the slightest hesitation aimed it at the light, pulled the trigger and bingo, out went the light! (Please note that although I like firearms I don't play silly buggers with real ones and nor do I carry them around with me. I'm daft, but not some kind of psycho.) I couldn't believe it: an absolute fluke, as even I wasn't as good a shot as that. The room erupted into howls of laughter and the next thing that we heard was Ron shouting, 'Oh shit! It's broken all over the side of my bed!' More laughter when he said: 'Now I'll have to clean it up and I can't see a sodding thing!'

Mick the roadie said: 'Well, get out of bed, you prat, and switch the light on!' And believe it or not that's just what he did. All you could hear was him cursing and yelling: 'Ouch, you bastards, that hurts!' We couldn't stop laughing but I yelled at him to jump back into bed and grabbed a spare blanket from one of the free beds and flung it over to him.

'Shut up dopey,' Jack said. 'Just get to sleep and we'll clear it up in the morning when it's light.' Apart from being confused (Ron's usual state of mind), he wasn't hurt. In fact the bulb when it broke had splattered in the recess of the door way and it was nowhere near the switch, so all that Ron suffered was cold feet and that was what was making him yell. My best snapshot ever and with a toy gun! Buffalo Bill and Annie Oakley eat your heart out. At least that is a true story and not one that I've invented to inflate myself.

Another fascinating work of fantasy was overheard by Graham, our drummer, whilst at a recording studio owner's dinner party. This one was very imaginative and occurred when for some reason Blodwyn Pig came up in the conversation. This individual, whose nickname is Barry the Wanker (says it all really), leaned over to the host and in Graham's earshot said to the guy: 'I have it on very reliable authority that Mick Abrahams stabbed someone to death years ago and got clean away with it!' Fortunately the guy he was telling the tale to knew me very well - we've been friends for years.

'What are you talking about?' he said.

Just then Graham leapt to my defence and said, 'Are you aware that I've worked with Mick for 16 years and I happen to know he is not the kind of character that you are portraying so I think you ought to keep your stupid mouth shut.'

I since found out that the same Barry the Wanker went on

to spread some lovely fairy tales about Martin Barre being a very violent and psychotic man! Two things should be noted about the content of these sorry lies. I don't like knives (I'm scared to butter bread for fear of cutting my fingers!). And Martin Barre is a terrific guy, gentle and mild-mannered and a very fine guitar player too. I do hope that people continue to invite Barry the Wanker to their dinner parties as he is great entertainment value for anyone who doesn't like Jethro Tull, Blodwyn Pig or enjoys listening to a pathological liar! Maybe he should set up in business as a Pathological-Liar-O-Gramme!

I have digressed a bit, but felt that certain things should be said.

We did some fantastic gigs with some great people such as B B King, The Who, the Allman Brothers and many others. We played an outdoor festival at the Columbia Bowl with The Who and Procul Harum to a crowd of around 40,000 people and it was fantastic, one of the best gigs that I can remember from that time. We just happened to be staying in the same Holiday Inn (everyone stayed at Holiday Inns for some reason or another) as all the other bands on the gig, which was not until the following day.

Chapter 36
Pigs, Hotels, Mooney and BJ

Now if there had ever been a recipe for potential disaster, this had to be a prime case. At around 2pm everyone had been boozing quite heavily and Keith Moon (an old stalwart occasional drinking buddy and all-round good guy) and B J Wilson (Procul Harum's drummer) were somewhat the worse for wear and decided that a swim would cool them down. The only hiccup being that they decided to dispense with the formality of a swimming cossie and dived off the top board at the pool stark bollock naked. Normally this would have caused no problem. If it had been late at night and they were the only ones in the pool, but unfortunately it was full of guests and there was some kind of convention of preachers from a state biblical college who were all congregating around the pool area for a quiet afternoon and they just didn't see the funny side of it. No sense of humour, some people!

The security guy came over and asked them to leave immediately and he was told to go forth and multiply in a non-biblical fashion. After some arguing and shouting on both sides they eventually retired to their rooms, which would have been okay but B J was still starkers and had passed out in a drunken stupor on the bed without drawing the curtains. He was obviously having some wonderful erotic dream because the next thing we heard was a scream from the general direction of his room. A Presbyterian minister and his wife and kids had just happened to walk along the landing and passing BJ 's room had noticed the door, windows, curtains and everything else open to be confronted by the lovely vision of a naked man lying face up on the bed with a raging hard on!

They must have called the cops, because the next thing we saw was about three or four very large policemen hauling poor old B J and Mooney away (apparently Mooney had come to B J's aid because he thought he was being kidnapped!). The last sound we heard before they were unceremoniously dumped in the police wagon was Mooney yelling for the British Consul and a fleet of gunboats. One of the many fun incidents on that tour and par for the course on most rock band tours, I guess. Having watched the iconic film Spinal Tap, I still think by comparison we were babes in arms! Needless to say we played some good music, met up with some really cool people and got through it all in one piece.

Chapter 37
Coming Back To Earth

Now here comes the sick part. Three days after I'd got home and was feeling rested and ready to rock once again, Andy Pyle (remember me saying earlier that he was always the selfish one in every band I'd ever been in with him) rang me to tell me the astounding news that Blodwyn Pig was going to continue minus myself! I was flabbergasted and angry to say the least. He went on to say how they'd all decided to dispense with me as my phobia of flying was not good for everyone's future and the band wouldn't continue to gain success unless I flew everywhere. I felt shat upon from a great height, betrayed and belittled.

Whilst these days I harbour no resentment or bad feelings to any of the guys for their actions, they had definitely made a really dumb decision, as I heard later that the band died on its arse every time they did a gig from that point on. Sadly for them they killed the whole thing about Blodwyn Pig without realising it. It was not my ego saying you'll never do this without me, but simply that I really knew what made the unit tick. I think Jack did too, but in hindsight he just got swept up in the melée. I had a conversation with Jack many years later when he admitted that they had made a major duff decision and that the main orchestrator of the uprising (so to speak) was none other than Andy! Sadly he was always looking out for his interests and his alone and shit stirring and suchlike seemed to be his stock in trade.

They recruited two new guys to replace me: Pete Banks on lead guitar (he was originally with Yes) and Barry Reynolds on rhythm guitar and vocals. A long time after the event, I did hear a tape of the stuff that they did and it sounded very weak and certainly nothing like the Blodwyn Pig that I had put together - and that's not sour grapes, it just didn't sound right. In fact, I was shattered that they had (in my opinion) ruined the band from a musical perspective as well as any future prospects. Both the guys that replaced me were good players but, with the greatest of respect to both of them, they did not suit the type of thing that Blodwyn Pig did. Anyway, the band known as Blodwyn Pig folded completely seven weeks after that event, so I feel that speaks volumes.

Incredibly, about a month later I received a call from Andy to ask me if I would consider getting back together with them. The conversation went something like this. 'Hi Mick, it's Andy. How are you doing?' I just found it hard to believe the cheek of the call, but I kept my temper for a few moments before he asked. 'Well Mick, I and the lads have had a serious talk about getting you to come back into the band.'

Great! Me being asked to rejoin my own band after being sacked: and when they found out they'd screwed up and it all fell apart; just simply ask me to rejoin. As you can imagine I was still seriously pissed off at them, so my answer was very straightforward and went along these lines. 'I've already formed another band, and I won't have time to play stupid games with you any more, so fuck off!' I then slammed the phone down, nearly breaking it in half. Enough said!

It took me a long while to forgive that piece of what I could only consider as foul treachery, but eventually I relented and let it go. Life's too short and I've learnt that the longer you hold on to grudges and hatred, the higher the risk of them becoming a consuming fire and working against you! It was yet another learning curve for me and in an odd way it was a positive part of my life's roller coaster education. I thought I had started to roll with the punches, but that was only the state of my mind at the time. There were still plenty more surprises around the next corner.

Chapter 38
Wommett and the Mick Abrahams Band

'

The day after I had that wretched phone call from Andy, I decided to form the Mick Abrahams Band. And from that point on, I decided to become somewhat more autocratic in my attitude towards the running of a band. I have, however, never been and never will be dictatorial in the hard-line sense of the word, because having worked under one dictatorship, I know that it can stifle any true potential for musical expression and eventually ends up causing bad feeling. Whilst I love the discipline of arranged parts of music, as songs for me must have a strong foundation and structure, I've always felt (rightly or wrongly) that freedom of expression in what you play is paramount, and that outlook still works for me to this day.

The story takes over exactly two days after my departure (forced retirement, sacking, call it what you will) from Blodwyn Pig. Somehow I was able to cast aside the bitterness, disappointment and anger. I decided that the only way forward at this point in time was simply to form another band and just get on with it all. The old thing about getting back on the horse!

Within two weeks I'd cobbled together some very different and most unlikely characters in the form of Ritchie Dharma (drums) Peter Fensome (bass) and a totally nutty classical violinist (John Darnborough). I decided to call the band Wommett, the name that Regimental Sergeant Major Cannon used to call me when I was a rank and file Gunner in the Royal Artillery during my army service, already covered in a previous chapter.

This name was later dropped in favour of the more simple working title of "The Mick Abrahams Band", (point of interest for the train spotters' brigade and something I have only recently found out by looking up the John Evan history page on the Internet is that Ritchie Dharma did most of the recording of the John Evan band's first album. He never mentioned it to me ever!).

We started rehearsing and it sounded different, but quite cool, so I took the band out on the road and again the reception was excellent. The one fly in the ointment was the manic fiddle player John. On the very first gig he completely forgot that we'd rehearsed certain parts of the songs as a fixed thing, leaving spaces for him and me to solo over. Instead of playing with the band, he suddenly went into "look how much I can play" mode and completely (to everyone's utter amazement) overrode and overplayed everything. Leaping to the front of the stage and jumping about like a whirling dervish, he just completely ignored everything we'd planned. Now don't get me wrong. I'm all for freedom of expression, but this was just bullshit. It seemed like every time he stepped on to a stage this monstrous alter ego appeared and proceeded to screw the show up. It was just not musical. In fact it was bloody awful!

So sadly after only two months with the band I was faced with the unpleasant task of giving poor John the boot! At that point in my life I had never had to sack anyone, and the fact that John was a really nice guy underneath all his quirky behaviour didn't make it any the easier. When I took him on one side to give him the bad news, instead of being angry, the poor sod just broke down into floods of tears. I think I'd rather he had called me a few names and told me to go and stuff myself, but this was something I found difficult to deal with.

To replace John I brought in Bob Sargeant on keyboards. I had met him along the way and seen him playing with the now legendary Newcastle band the Junco Partners. Bob fitted in the band well as we were now becoming tighter and more aggressive. Pete Fensome decided it was time for him to leave and pursue a solo songwriting career, as once again he wanted to do softer more pop-type songs. I take my hat off to him as we are still great friends and he's written some lovely stuff over the years too. To replace him I brought in Walt Monaghan on bass, who had previously played with Free and If.

Chapter 39
The MA Band Shapes Up

The band started to pick up momentum and was playing well, and we went into Air London studios in Oxford Street with a whole new batch of new songs to record the first MA band album, produced by Chris Thomas and I had a great time recording it. The songs on this album were about my own experiences of the past and present and my feelings about thing in general, but still an underlying influence of blues-infused rock but this time with the extra vocal power of Bob and Walt. That made a very pleasant change as up until that point I had always been the only vocalist in Blodwyn Pig and vocal harmonies was a good way of putting colour into the songs. There was plenty that had built up inside me; good and bad. There was a lot to get on with and I found this time very constructive and very musical. We worked very hard to get a tight-sounding band and it started to show.

Apart from the work there was the usual ligging and fooling around, which has seemed to accompany every band I've ever worked with (I wonder why). One peculiar incident comes to mind (perhaps even in the way of a confession). One evening we'd had a break for a little libation and a curry (Bob Sargeant's idea, but the tight-fisted git never coughed up any money towards it). As it was Bob's turn to do some overdubbing I was temporarily without something to occupy myself, so guess what? Yes, I went across the road to the local boozer and got totally paralytic pissed. I stumbled back to the studios after a few hours, but things were somewhat hazy and I was dying for a pee! As the lights were all out in the rest of the building I fumbled and fell about looking for the bog, but to no avail. Suddenly, joy! I thought I'd found the right room Where's the bloody light switch? My fuddled mind cried out, and I started to panic a bit, so I just felt my way round in the gloom desperately seeking the urinal, and unable to wait any longer, I relieved myself and staggered back to the main studio.

Now all I can remember was waking up the next morning to be told that I'd had a riotous evening and would I now ring everyone up and apologise for my behaviour. I found out later that I had passed out in the control room after insisting that it was the curry that had made me vomit all over the reception desk on my way into the building and the fact that I'd emptied a fire extinguisher down the front of Bob Sargeant's trousers was merely because I was putting a cigarette out that I'd dropped on him. I was in the doghouse the next day, as late that previous evening some uncouth person had urinated in one of the offices of George Martin. I don't know to this day who committed that foul deed, I'm sure it wasn't me, but how could I know? So if it was me that pissed in your desk drawer, Sir George, I'm extremely sorry but I was incapable of aim or judgment at that time and I hope the stains came out alright!

I'd soon returned to everyone's good graces and the album got finished in good time and, although it didn't bust any records by going into the top ten albums listings, it still continues to sell well to this day. I think that this album was far superior to the second effort *At Last*, which was one of my least favourites. However, the band continued to work all around the UK and Europe again, did good business and we still went down a storm every time we played. Most of the tours were done by road and rail and boat, which suited me down to the ground, but the old paranoia about flying in airliners hadn't abated, so we didn't ever visit the USA, which was a pity because I think they would have liked what we had to offer. The two favourite songs of mine on that album are *Greyhound Bus* and *Big Queen*, which were both about the modes of travel that avoided taking planes.

Chapter 40
More MA Band Mayhem

Another ridiculous incident was when the Mick Abrahams Band played at yet another of those dinner jacket college-type gigs, this time somewhere in Wiltshire. The usual hospitality was laid on for the performers and just for a change the entertainment committee organiser was quite a reasonable and affable chap. We went on stage at around 10pm (a much more civilized time) to do what should have been an hour's set. Walt and Ritchie were pissed as rats and were wobbling about all over the stage, but I counted the first number (*Greyhound Bus*) in and everything kicked off well.

Around the fourth number it became apparent that Walt had got quite a few large bottles of beer stashed behind his bass stack and was topping up constantly between tunes or even in the middle of them. As a consequence he and Ritchie seemed to be in competition with each other to see who could down the most beer and make each other laugh. As it happened, it was one of those gigs where nearly all the audience seems to be either pissed out of their brains or high as kites on some substance or other. Anyway the mirth and general vibe amongst the guys was really infectious and after the fourth song Walt staggered up to the mike and announced in his loud and bolshie Cockney voice: 'I'd like to do a blues song for you now.'

Well it wasn't a problem for us to just drop in a straightforward slow 12-bar blues tune every now and then, so that's exactly what we did. The first 12 instrumental bars were fine, but Walt's impromptu lyrics left something to be desired as he belted out a superb rough-voiced rendition of his latest composition *Oh Baby, I Wanna Fuck Your Dog!* We couldn't believe our ears but as I signalled frantically to the sound engineer to turn Walt's mike off he disappeared behind his bass stack. I took over the vocal and sang some more appropriate lyrics (this time replacing the offensive word 'dog' with 'cat'! Only kidding!) But we were all still in shock and hysterics at Walt's outburst and I could hardly sing because I was in tears of laughter.

When it came time for Bob to do an organ break for 24 bars or so, I turned around to see Ritchie barely able to keep upright on his drum stool for laughing. Walt couldn't be seen, but he was still playing so I wondered just what the hell was going on. I soon found the source of Ritchie's mirth and now Bob had nearly stopped playing too as he had seen what Ritchie could see and I couldn't. Unbelievably Walt had crept behind his bass stack (and how he did it I will never fathom out) had dropped his trousers and underpants and was taking a massive dump whilst somehow keeping three notes in play. I couldn't play for laughing. The whole thing just fell apart and we all literally fell about pissed and helpless. Our roadie Mick came to Walt's rescue and pulled him to his feet and somehow managed to get his shit covered pants and trousers back on, and with a look of disgust on his face (and who could blame him) said: 'Aarrgghh, you dirty bastard! You can clean that up afterwards cause sure as eggs are eggs I ain't doing it!'

All this time, the audience just kept dancing and jigging about as if it were all part of the act and how we managed to play for another half hour I will never know, but we did (We wrapped a large curtain around Walt that Mick found or nicked from our dressing room.) We finally left the stage to thunderous applause.

'Aren't we going to do an encore?' asked the dishevelled, drunken, crap-stained Walt.

'Yeah sure,' I said. 'Why don't you just go back on stage on your own, vomit on the first two rows of the audience and finish it all off by pissing into the mixing desk on the side of the stage and give the punters a beautiful coloured electric light show?' I really think if I'd have pushed the suggestion, he would have done it too! We just laughed all the way home. Naturally, Walt had passed out in the van by then and didn't remember a thing about it (or so he said) the next day. Rock'n'roll, eh?

Chapter 41
The Same Old Crap!

We continued gigging around Europe and the UK and did good business. During a short European tour with Ten Years After we played the Montreux Jazz & Blues Festival. During the afternoon we all took a stroll along the picturesque shores of Lake Geneva and browsed in the curiosity and gift shops which were in abundance. The fly in this ointment was that (I never mentioned this before, but the story is just too good to waste) Ritchie Dharma, our mad drummer, had a serious problem: he was a self-confessed and very prolific kleptomaniac. He just couldn't go anywhere without stealing something. If we were in a garage shop or café or anywhere there were things that he could nick, he would. We all distanced ourselves physically from him like the plague when we were out in a group as we knew he couldn't help himself and we didn't want to get dragged into - or worse, blamed for - his thieving habit!

It was a bright sunny afternoon and we all knew that he was itching to nick something, so we kept our distance from him and when he entered a gift shop we just kept walking slowly onward. To give you an idea of Ritchie's oddness, picture this. A tubby Indian guy (he was born in Bombay) with a very large black leather flat gaucho hat, black sunglasses, a full-length black leather Gestapo coat and a constantly lit Gauloise cigarette. This was what he liked to call his thieving kit! Inside the long leather coat which he had purchased at a flea market somewhere in Amsterdam, he had persuaded his long suffering wife to sew a series of hooks and special pockets for hiding his ill-gotten gains.

Off he walked into the shop looking very furtive. He was actually trying to look cool and mysterious, but we all knew what he was about to do! Within three minutes a breathless voice sounded from behind us.

'Hang on guys; wait for me.' He caught up with us. Walt was the first to speak.

'All right, Dick Friggin' Turpin, what have you nicked now, you thieving git?'

'Oh, nothing much,' said Ritchie with a really evil grin all over his face.

'Don't believe you,' said Walt and started to pat his coat down like a cop searching a suspect. As he did it there was a sound that I will never forget and one that still cracks me up laughing every time I hear it. "Cuckoo, cuckoo". Ritchie opened his coat to reveal his prize and there still chiming and cuckooing away was a large cuckoo clock, hanging from one of his secret hooks. Unbelievable! We all just fell about laughing, not that we condoned what he got up to, but the thought of how he had got such cheek to just walk in the shop and steal a very large, fully-working clock from under the nose of the unfortunate shop owner. The rest of us quickened our pace and left him out of breath with the sounds of the cuckoo clock still chiming underneath his coat.

When we arrived back at the hotel later I asked him what he had done with it and why he did it. He said: 'I dumped it in a bin and it's just something I can't help doing.' I told him to seek treatment, but he said he enjoyed it too much. A great guy, a great and ferocious drummer and a good mate, but I kept well away from him when I suspected he might be at it. In the evening we had a fabulous time. The gig was great, the audience amazing and the hospitality second to none. We all came home tired and happy that we'd played some good music to some great audiences and then went our separate ways and had a couple of well-deserved weeks off.

Chapter 42
At Last

The Mick Abrahams Band did a one-off appearance on Top of the Pops as they had included what they called the album band slot. We played a song called *Why Do You Do Me This Way*, which was co written with Bob from the first album, *A Musical Evening With*. A good song and probably more bluesy than the rest of the material from that album. Personally I thought that *Greyhound Bus* was a better and stronger song and much better suited to a show like Top of the Pops, but the powers that be seemed to know better and the song bombed. The crowd liked it though; just not the BBC or our management. I enjoyed doing *Top of the Pops* as I had done the show just once before with Blodwyn Pig with our first single record attempt *Same Old Story*. I liked the dancers too and always had a thing about Pan's People, a lovely group of ladies who gave me great pleasure to watch. Yes, I did say watch!

The next task was to record what I personally consider as the infamous *At Last* album. We were back in Air London studios again, once more under the guidance of Chris Thomas. By this time I'd kissed and made up with Jack Lancaster and asked him to join the band. It was nice to have the colour of another instrument in the band again and, although Jack did a sterling job, I'd started to feel that some of the songs were weak and felt that Chris had lost interest in the band generally. One of the major problems was that Bob had become increasingly more interested in trying to get as many of his songs on the album as he possibly could presumably to further his impending solo career, and whilst he had certainly written a couple of good tunes which sat nicely in the album, the rest of it was very pop, which didn't suit the style at all. It was made worse by his constant whingeing attitude about money and the whole thing. He really was starting to get on my tits as he was like a dog with a bone, and good player though he was it had once again degenerated into shit stirring and petty arguments. The rot had set in once again for me. I'd trodden this path before and I was just pissed off with it all.

I knew it had gone beyond the point where I could put up with the nonsense all over again, so I just stuck with the same line-up for around another two months and then after some deliberation decided to whittle the band down to a three-piece outfit to see if we could find some new energy to inject into the old dog! Ritchie, Jack, and Bob went off to pastures new and we all parted on good terms. Bob wanted to be a pop star, but ended up as a very good producer and became highly sought after during the eighties, producing quite a few big pop bands of that era. Jack got married for the umpteenth time and moved to America to do a lot of writing and production for the Hanna-Barbera animation company. Ritchie told us that he was going to open a string of nightclubs and hopefully take over the prime position of Peter Stringfellow, but I think he ended up running a chicken farm for a short time just to fulfil his odd sexual proclivities and to cure his thieving habit! Just kidding. Walt Monaghan still being the aggressive little rocker: said: yes; let's give it a go as a three piece, and so we asked the late Wilgar Campbell of Rory Gallagher fame to play drums and fill Ritchie's vacant slot.

Poor old Ritchie made me promise to write a chapter about him if I ever got round to writing this book and I told him that if I ever did, it would be just as he would have wished: The truth that he was a total nut job! Ritchie suffered from poor health for a long time and sadly he died a few years back. I didn't hear anything from him for a while and didn't know how to get in touch, until his son Jason contacted me by email through my website. He is now over 35 and a very tough, fit and capable ex-Royal Marine Commando who runs a diving school. I'm in touch with him still and the first time he had ever seen his dad play was when I showed him a video of us doing the Top of the Pops show that I just mentioned. He is a great credit to our old mate Ritchie and I miss seeing the old loony, who used to turn up unannounced at gigs every now and then. I would always know when he was in the audience, as usually someone from the venue would come over to me and hand me a home-made calling card which was simply a disgusting pornographic picture with the text overlaid. Ritchie Dharma. Drumming, House Painting and Chicken Fornication! Seeing it never failed to make me fall about. I miss him still.

Chapter 43
God's Hand on Me

Around this time I suddenly found religion (I think that's how people describe it) and became a member of an Evangelical Church. Yes, honestly! I'd been brought up in the Christian faith from a very early age. I was even a choirboy and altar boy in my youth. I don't know how it all happened, but you know what they say. You might not be taking too much notice of God but you can bet your boots that he always has his hand on you and he certainly did in my case. After my initial acceptance of God's presence in my life the people that I got involved with were sincere and genuinely decent people, together with a couple of exceptional people came to my aid when I needed help the most and are still very dear and close friends to this day.

Some (not all) of the others involved in this particular church did tend to have rather a blinkered outlook on everything else, some of them even to the point of fanaticism, and it didn't wear well after a while with me, as I am a very open-minded person. This was also the point where my marriage to Stephanie had started to show strain (I think mostly due to my lifestyle as much as her own hang-ups) and I was certainly very stressed out about the way everything had been going for me and the business generally. Also my faith in people was being sorely put to trial and that didn't go down well either. However, what that renewed baptism of faith did do was to leave me with reinvigorated spiritual strength and the feeling that not everything in the world was as bad as I had previously seen it. Or maybe I'd been given the ability to deal with those things with a more positive attitude. So, while I am still (and always will be) a confirmed believer, I just can't get to grips with the accepted regime of a zealously organised church. Whilst I accept that it works for a number of reasons and on a number of levels for some people, for me there is still too much hypocrisy, in some cases unacceptable fundamentalism, fanatical fervour and far too much dogma.

I believe in love, tolerance, goodness and kindness to our fellow creatures regardless of who or what they are and that's what the Bible teaches, as do most of the holy books I've read, but like all the other books, it's abused and misinterpreted by man as a way for getting what they want for their own selfish purposes and that's not for me. Whatever my personal beliefs are, I am still firmly on this world and not the next and I am still very much a human person, simply faithful and not a religious crackpot. I love Christ, but not creepy Christian nutters who pray about whether they should go to the loo or not. And, believe me, there are some about: I've met them. My answer to those people is simple. Just go when you need to, my dears! It's nature's way of telling you that things are about to get messy otherwise. Here endeth the lesson!

Chapter 44
Major Changes 1974/5

The MA band still continued to tour, but we never got round to recording a studio album. The only recordings of that time are the *Live in Madrid* album, which was taken from the mixing desk in the M &M club in Madrid Spain, which I must admit, does have a bit of life about it and it was probably a good note on which to hang my axe up for a while. Admittedly we did have a good little unit going, but it was never destined to do anything. Doug Darcy, our manager (dare I call him that?), just really didn't give a toss and to all intents and purpose had given up on me. Not that I blame him really as, after all, me, John Bonham and Stan Webb did leave him stranded on that traffic island trussed up like a turkey so it's not that surprising really, is it?

I think this is where I came in.

This was the point in time that saw me putting the guitar away in the loft. And the very next day I went out and bought myself a second-hand, very old-fashioned (but lovely) Ford Popular, a roof rack, a cheap set of aluminium ladders, a large plastic bucket, a few rolls of scrim (tech speak for window cleaning rag!), a pair of overalls and drove around a few estates and canvassed them to see who wanted their windows cleaned every two weeks. Within a fortnight I had loads of customers as apparently window cleaners were in short supply because no one seemed to want to do it.

I loved it. I didn't have to worry about anything but turning up and washing folk's windows, taking a reasonable few bob off them, then going home at five o'clock to spend time with my young son, Alex, and my wife Stephanie. For a while it was relaxing to say the least. Around the first two months of Blodwyn Pig forming I got married, just like my Mum said normal young men of my age should do. 'You should think of settling down with a nice young lady like Stephanie,' she said, in that all-knowing voice of hers. She was always right about everything and would never be proven wrong by man, beast or even God himself. She had a very self-righteous attitude about most things, but in her heart of hearts she meant well. She was, however, blissfully unaware that the kind of lifestyle that goes with the territory of being in a couple of famous rock bands and the behaviour patterns that accompany it.

Whilst I was never inclined to hard drugs or excessive amounts of alcohol, I certainly enjoyed the pleasures of cannabis, a pint or two and a drop of scotch every now and then, and definitely the company of a few wayward women. Oddly enough when I was Jethro Tull's lead guitar player, I hardly drank, certainly didn't smoke dope or anything else (with the exception of cigarettes) and wasn't much bothered about extraneous crumpet either. That all changed when Blodwyn Pig began, and even more so when we started visiting the States. It was only then that I became more of a party animal and joined in all the misbehaviour that I could!

At this point in my life things had changed beyond all recognition. The bubble hadn't just burst in my life; it seemed to have taken the form of a giant nuclear explosion that engulfed me and then spat me out again. I have never been one to stay down for long when I've been in tough situations. I always get up and I always will until they screw the lid on me. It's in my blood not to give up and although I go about it in odd ways, at no point during any of my music career, even when things were at their worst ebb, did I ever feel sorry for myself and I never will. I have had a great life (and still am having one, thank God) full of much love, countless blessings, great friends and a richness that sometimes defies imagination. I would not swap one minute of any of it because at no point have I felt hard done to. It's left me with a good perspective about life, people and what is what.

Well, the window cleaning was fine, but it soon became apparent that this was a short-term measure on the road back to what I considered reality or "normality". I had my hair cut as short as my vanity would allow, but in spite of this I was constantly recognised around Dunstable, where I was living at this time. I'm sure that some people thought I was either doing it for a gag or I'd lost the plot altogether, but both theories were wrong. It was like a form of therapy if you will and it worked to some degree. I was blessed with a son who I immediately named Alexis (after my dear friend and mentor Alexis Korner), who is now a wonderful guitar player and writer and, at the time of writing, 35 years old and just like my younger son, Nick. (He came along later when I married my second wife, Kate, and is now 27 years old and works in visual design.) We are really great mates and although I'm their Dad I still consider that being with them is just like being around your best buddies and that's the way it will always be. Gangs of fun.

My marriage to Stephanie was by now showing more signs of strain and even my new-found faith did not seem to help in the least. In fact, if anything it seemed to be more destructive and this is where my remarks about some of the type of folk that I got involved with are relevant. Some people are blinded by the way that they think things ought to be; or how they personally interpret their view of other people's problems. Marriages are probably the most difficult for them to deal with. None of them and most especially the supposed spiritual leader of the church that I was a member of just did not want to know or even seem to care. In fact this charismatic leader couldn't even be bothered to knock on my door and have a chat or a cup of tea with me. He simply passed by my house without even as much as a glance. It was fortunate that deep down in my heart I knew that God cared, even if he didn't have the bottle to admit that he didn't!

I just simply and honestly believe that Stephanie was just not meant to be with someone like myself and sadly it ended in divorce for us. I was more heart-broken about leaving young Alex behind, but I swore a solemn oath to my ex wife, to Alex and God almighty that I would always love and cherish him, maintain and look after him no matter what and that has held true to this day, for which again I am profoundly grateful.

Between the window cleaning rounds I somehow found time to go for a swim every morning at our local pool. I was a keen swimmer in my younger days (three sports I seemed to excel at were swimming, shooting, and judo). I always hated football, athletics and the like but suddenly got the yearning to become fit and active once more.

Within a couple of months of my visits I became friendly with the manager there, a nice chap called John Sharpe, who took me on one side and said: 'Look, you are obviously a good swimmer and you told me you did lifesaving when you were a kid and you're in here every morning. Why don't you re-take your lifesaving and survival qualifications and come and work here five mornings a week?' I thought, Yeah, why not? It's free exercise and I'd get paid for it too.

I cleaned my last window and passed the cleaning round on to another deserving chap and that was that. I passed all my qualifications with flying colours right up to gaining the

Royal Life Saving Society's award of distinction. I still swim regularly to this day and have never lost the fun aspect of it even after all this time.

So, there I was with a regular, normal job and a small but reasonable income. It has to be said that, unbelievably, I seemed to earn more money at the time than the pitiful wages that Chrysalis paid into my bank on a weekly basis!

The job carried on for three or four months and then three things happened that were to change my ever-twisting fates around yet again. The first was that I just happened to be looking around a brand new sports complex that was under building completion in Dunstable (and was simply being nosey, I guess) when a voice from behind me said: 'Can I help you?'

'Oh sorry,' I said, 'I was just interested in the pool. It looks pretty good. When will it be completed?'

'Do you work in the industry?' asked the guy.

'Yes,' I replied. 'I'm currently working at another pool a few miles away, but this one is right on my doorstep.'

He then asked about my qualifications and stunned me by asking 'How would you like to take the job of pool manager?'

'Yes I'd like that very much," I said (I had no clue how to be a pool manager, but why not when the chance is there?).

'When can you start?'

'Well, I'd have to give a week's notice.'

'Fine, that's that sorted then,' he said. 'Come and see me tomorrow and we'll get the details and paperwork done.'

So I parted from my old job with good wishes from my work mates and remarks like jammy bastard! and lucky sod! I then moved up in the world of leisure and swimming pool management. I was actually very good at, learnt a lot about the industry and even got two commendations and made the local newspapers for saving a couple of lives or something, but all simply part of what I was trained to do, because I certainly ain't no hero, no way!

The next life-changing event was that I met my lovely wife Kate and, to cut a long story short (I've been married to her for 33 years now), fell madly in love and knew that I'd found a true soul mate. It was very difficult as I was already married to someone. Cheating and being sneaky are not my general way of doing things, but you know, these things do happen and being only human, things took their course and I ended up divorcing Stephanie and a year later, married Kate. It was an odd time and sometimes hard emotionally for everyone concerned and I wouldn't recommend divorce as a regular practice. Once is enough, thanks!

Anyway things eventually turned out well as good things always should do and we were blessed with another son, Nick. The great thing was, and still is, that there is great love and friendship between both my sons, and when people ask me to this day why there is a big age difference between them (Alex is now 35 and Nick is now 27), I simply laugh and say 'We watched a hell of a lot of television for a while!'

The third event occurred after only six months into my supposed "normal life". I was getting more and more frustrated that I was not getting any artistic fulfilment especially from a musical perspective. I still had a head full of music, you see, and as I reached into the loft one evening to get a suitcase or some such item, my eyes rested on the guitar case which had started to gather a bit of dust. I gingerly pulled it down, dusted it off and opened it. I knew right from the very moment I set my eyes on it that I just had to pick it up and play. The strings were a slight bit rusty, but play it I did - and did so for at least three hours before swearing that I would never put it away again. You see, I had come to the realisation that all the crap that I had been through was absolutely nothing to do with music. Music was and will always be the true heart of me. It was simply that I was just not mature or emotionally strong enough to withstand the bullshit that surrounds the industry. So there I was having gone through all these changes but still with music uppermost in my heart and mind.

We did do a very brief reformation of Blodwyn Pig around 1974, this time with good old Clive Bunker playing drums. It strangely enough was a lot tighter than the original band, but that spark that we had from day one had gone. I did enjoy the brief encounter, although it only lasted six months. We had some odd management with some funny ideas and it just didn't work for me. We did a few gigs, even one at the grand old Marquee Club and a couple of radio shows. I even remember Dave Dee doing a couple of demo tracks with us down at Elstree Studios. I think it went well, but after I'd done my guitar and vocals I fell amongst thieves so to speak in the studio bar and got sidetracked by a whole bottle of Southern Comfort. In fact I was so comforted that the only recollection of the rest of the evening was waking up (or rather being woken up by Jack and Clive who had been looking everywhere for me and finally found me curled up unconscious in the orchestral studio's grand piano)! Thankfully they got me into a car and carted me off home to bed, where I passed out again for another eight hours. I do love recording! I wonder whatever happened to the final takes. Sorry Dave, I've always thought you were a good bloke!

The next life-changing event was that for no particular reason I turned up at the London Gliding Club on Dunstable Downs one bright morning, walked into the office and asked if they took people up in a glider just to see what it was like. Don't ask me why, but I've always been impetuous, and that morning was no exception. A pleasant chap, who I think was called John Hawkins, told me that, yes, they regularly did air experience flights and, as luck would have it, for the princely sum of £15 I could take a flight with him almost immediately. I probably thought he was going to tell me to come back later or tomorrow or something that would let me off the hook. I'd dabbled with the idea of trying out what I considered the most dangerous form of flying (no engine you see!) for some time, and that's why I was there, to see if it would cure me of my phobia of flying in airliners. I'd been in big helicopters and light aircraft before and they didn't bother me as badly as commercial airliners for some reason or another.

Within five minutes of me stammering 'yes, I'd love to do it now,' and parting with my 15 quid, I was being strapped into the cockpit of an ASK 13 Schliecher training glider and shown the controls. I was seriously nervous, but for some odd reason there was something peaceful about the beautiful surroundings and John's calm, matter-of-fact manner that put me at ease. He climbed in the back seat, pulled down the canopy and all of a sudden the tow rope attached to the small Piper Cub tow-plane in front of us became taut. We were off!

I hadn't much time to think about it, but the next thing I knew we were 5,000 feet above Dunstable Downs with the most amazing view of the countryside. John pulled a lever down by his side and the towing cable was released and the tow plane banked off to the right and made its way back to the airfield. The incredible feeling I had was one of absolute peace. There was no noise except the whistling of the wind past the aircraft. It was a truly amazing moment for me.

John started to coax me with the controls by saying things like 'Can you feel what the ailerons are doing?' and 'this is how we bank and turn the aircraft.' I was soaked in nervous sweat, but managed to take in most of what he was saying and held the controls gingerly in my hands. 'Can you feel that?' he asked me.

'Yes, I replied.

'Well, you've been flying the aircraft for nearly three minutes now,' he informed me. SHIT! (I think I nearly did too!) I could hardly believe that I was doing this, but there I was; actually in control of this thing. To cut a long story short, I don't think I would ever make a half reasonable pilot (even though I did take a few more lessons), as my coordination with the controls leaves something to be desired. But in my overactive imagination I would like to think that I could actually take over the controls of a Jumbo 747 if all the pilots died of some strange poisoning or were killed by terrorists, and land safely with the help of ground control, just like Kurt Russell did in the movie *Executive Decision*. Perhaps not, really, but as you probably by now have got the idea of how my very vivid imagination works, you'll know that it's simply a fantasy of mine and I'd rather not have it happen! I really liked and preferred the film. It did, however, get me through my worst fear and nowadays I usually take a plane as opposed to a train or boat. It's a lot quicker and cheaper too!

Chapter 45
Getting Back At It

I certainly did miss certain bits about the music business, like the touring and recording, but I was still playing regularly and earning a living. Young Nick was growing up and had started school and married life and its domestic comforts had their compensations, so things generally weren't all that bad. During the next few years I did all manner of things to earn a living and keep my mind off being on the road and touring and everything that goes with it.

I drove a truck, I sold second hand cars, I even sold life assurance for a while and, without blowing my own trumpet too much, I was pretty good at all of them! But nothing could replace the fact that I always have been a guitar player first and foremost and in December 1988 fate played a hand in making a decision to start me off playing full-time once again. This was the time in my life that I was on a quite serious fitness kick. I had taken up the only ball game I have ever been interested in or was half reasonably skilled at. Squash!

One winter's evening after a really tough game I was in the squash club bar having a beer or two when the manager casually asked me, why couldn't I put a special one-off band together and play the New Year's Eve party at the club? He knew who I was and my past track record and even had a couple of my albums. I wasn't about to give him his money back though!

It might just have been the beer talking, but I simply said, 'Yeah, all right, why not? If you would really like me to do something special I could put Blodwyn Pig back together just for the night.'

'That would be incredible,' he said, and off I went wondering what the hell I'd just committed myself to. I never renege on a promise and the next day I rang the late great Dick Heckstall-Smith (I knew Dick from way back and he'd play at the opening of a cornflakes box if you asked him!). I roped in Andy Pyle and Clive Bunker and another old mate from the Toggery Five days, Bernie Hethrington, to complete the line-up. I finally booked another pal that I'd been gigging with on a regular basis, Bruce Boardman, to play piano and complete the scenario. We even had a couple of rehearsals and it sounded really cool! That gig was what started it all over again for me and I'm thankful that it did, because from that point I knew clearly that all I wanted to do was make good music again. Within two weeks the news had spread that I had completely reformed a brand new, streamlined version of Blodwyn Pig. Funny how news like that travels so fast, but travel it did and within the next few weeks my phone rang off the hook.

Again fate playing its odd game reared its magical head. I was selling life assurance for a major company; and doing quite well at it, at least financially, but the truth was that I was truly bored out of my mind with it after a while and looking for an excuse to get out. The problem here was that I had by now acquired a nice house, a couple of cars and all the trappings of a successful life assurance salesman. (The company gave us various grand titles such as Financial Advisor or Consultant. All bullshit really: I was just a good salesman.) I had also acquired a substantial mortgage and other large debts to go with it all.

Looking back on my time doing that job. I took it on initially because believed that it would simply be almost part-time to bolster my meagre income as a musician and that's how I saw it for quite a long time. In truth it worked in completely the opposite way. The more commission I made from selling the company's products the more money I was earning and of course, spending! There came a point when I could only manage to play a couple of gigs a month as I was so tied up with the other things. As most of the gigs I was playing were either medium to small pubs or the occasional charity bash, it became harder to weigh one against the other. That old saying about follow your heart is still for me - the truest saying that I've ever heard, because it's simply gut-wrenching to do something you get no true satisfaction or pleasure from and just simply earn loads of money. Nothing wrong with money; it's how you get it and how you use it. I've at least now learnt that lesson. Although I am currently waiting for my first cheque for a few million quid, which I know will arrive soon as this book will prove.

In reality I am probably the richest kid on the block. I've got a great family, great kids and relations and genuine friends who would do anything for me as I would for them, so tell me how am I doing so far?

Yeah, I know!

Chapter 46
The Second Rebirth

More and more gig offers kept coming and two things started me back on the musical yellow brick road once again. The first was I had overspent and overextended myself financially and had a couple of serious setbacks with sales in general, too boring to go into detail about but the long and short of it is that I (like a few thousand others at that exact same time) was bankrupt! Gangs of fun being a financial consultant! I've always known how to make money and I'm good at it. The main downfall in my case is that I'm generous to a fault and haven't got a clue how to hold on to it! I'm still learning though and it is getting better.

I don't recall being too stressed out about the situation at that time with the exception of my family being my greater concern. My oldest son Alex was now living in Brighton with his mum and things were OK with them but I was concerned about Nick having to move schools and the general upheaval that I had caused. We put together a plan to get us out of the mire and it was quite simple really. My wife Kate had always been a teacher and now as Nick was around nine years old she was able to take on a full-time job. The first job she got offered was at the very same school where Nick was, so that cured a lot of logistical problems. The official receivers took our house away and we moved into temporary rented accommodation which was very pleasant and just about affordable and I started doing a few gigs every week to put bread on the table.

Oddly, having lost what to some would seem everything, I

didn't view it that way at all. In truth, for me it was like regaining everything, It became a better and somewhat less stressful life without the worry of having to think how many sales I would have to make that week to cover the mortgage and all the other expenses. I didn't have any money in the bank, but my family didn't go short.

Musically, things were getting really exciting again for me. I was playing exactly what I wanted, I didn't have a manager or a record company telling me what to do and where to go and when I finally got to the point where I couldn't avoid dealing with some of the creeps that still exist in the recording industry, I adopted a simple policy whereby if they didn't give me what I knew was fair and proper I just took the deal elsewhere. I am still acutely aware that I have been turned over a few times in the course of things. My view is now this. I try to get the most out of what they are offering for a record deal with the knowledge that they will always try it on and, of course, always in their favour. Once the price has been agreed I then feel that that's that, let's move on to the next thing and see how we do. However, I have always retained all my publishing rights and always will, as the Performing Rights Society and MCPS are always in my corner looking after that aspect and so far I've had no problems. I'm a lifelong member also of the Musicians Union and on a couple of recent occasions the Musicians Benevolent Society have come to my aid with medical problems that otherwise would have gone ignored, delayed and possibly not even treated. I even wrote a song recently which was on the Can't Stop Now album and its title, a bit tongue in cheek, was GBNHS. Blues. You can thank our last Prime Minister and our current faker for that one! Did I say faker? Sorry, I meant something entirely different, because we mustn't be rude to our country's leaders now, must we?

Chapter 47
Modern Times

The last 15 years or so have been such a lot of fun. The initial reincarnation of Blodwyn Pig whittled down with the parting on good terms with the manic but lovely Dick-Heckstall Smith or, as some of the less reverent members of the band called him, Dick Oxtail Soup or Dick Hacksaw Smith! A great guy and a truly original player was Dick and I was greatly saddened by his recent death. Bernie Hetherington was only ever in the band for the opening night and he decided once was enough and that was that. I still see Bernie from time to time and we have a beer or two and try to put the world to rights!

Dick's place was taken over by a fiery tenor sax player called Gordon Murphy who was a music teacher at an American school in London, but originally from Biloxi, Mississippi. A real good lad and a great visual asset to the band as he is a very large and imposing guy and his presence added weight to the band (no pun intended Gordon). We immediately nicknamed him Mississippi Murphy and he was very popular with the fans. Gordon had too many other commitments with his regular teaching job and so, sadly we parted company amicably after a year. Bruce Boardman is a very gifted jazz pianist and also probably one of the finest exponents of boogie and stride piano and we still keep in touch and do the occasional gig or demo show together. He was not cut out for the type of band that Blodwyn is as a whole, but did some sterling work on a few tracks on two early 90s albums.

Clive had a better job offer which he just couldn't turn down and so he departed for a while and we are still doing projects together here and all over Europe to this present day (I don't think we can live without each other) and having fun every time. Graham Walker replaced Clive on drums and we've become good mates since the late 80s. Graham is still a regular member of the MA band and Blodwyn Pig, a great groove drummer, totally reliable, solid and very easy to work with. For a while Bruce was replaced by Dave Lennox (or Lummox as we nicknamed him) on keyboards. Dave is a fine player but a crisis in waiting. His gear was always breaking down, as was his car and sometimes, I feared, his sanity! Dave's saving grace was that every time he went into one of his daft spats about nothing in general, mostly drug-induced I think, he would do one of two things, he'd just crack everyone up laughing because he was being so stupid and couldn't see it, or just piss everyone off to the point of wanting to leave him asleep in a hotel room far away somewhere and not bother to try to find him again! He was still a good solid member of the Blod fraternity and contributed some great stuff to the songs during his time with us.

There is a great story about Dave and his general excesses. Around 1997 we had done a short run of gigs in the West Country and Cornwall. The last of these was the White Horse at Launceston. A full house and a good crowd - and a good time was had by all, with the exception of Dave who just before we were due to play swallowed what he laughingly called some kind of herbal tablets. Yeah, really Dave, we all believed you! He'd had a few pints of the local brew and, being a true blue, life-long dope smoker was quite laid back at first, but we noticed that a quarter of the way into the set he became very animated and started jumping up and down and thrashing around wildly every time he had a solo break. It was quite worrying at first because we all though he was cracking up or had been taken ill. After the gig he would just not stop talking and couldn't keep still. He consumed a few more pints and I'm fairly certain took some more of his supposed "herbal remedy". We left him in the bar still talking to anyone who would listen and we were told the next morning that he'd finally ran out of steam and, after talking to himself for a while, collapsed in a heap and had to be put to bed by the kind landlord and his wife.

Needless to say Dave didn't appear at the breakfast table and we had a long journey ahead of us all. Dave and I had travelled together in my car and the other guys in their respective vehicles. I went to his room to wake him and found him still dressed from the previous night and looking like the very spectre of death!

'Come on, you dozy toss pot,' I said and managed to kick his arse out of bed so that we could get going as it was 9.30am and I needed to get back for a solo gig that evening. There was much groaning and moaning and protests.

'Can't I stay in bed till around midday?' he pleaded.

'Balls,' I said, 'we have to get going, so haul your sad ass into the car and let's hit the road!'

I really should have just left him there because although the roads were not congested and the weather was quite warm and sunny, during the drive Dave managed to be sick in the car at least three times. I stopped at a motorway café and got him a few plastic bags so that he could throw up to his heart's content as I'd already stopped twice to clean the muck out of the car and I was getting pissed off with it to say the least. On the whole of that journey he managed to vomit at least twenty times, stop the car the same amount of times and fill the bag to overflowing three times. The final stop was when he asked yet again: 'Please, Mick, just let me out of the car and let me have a lay down on this grassy lawn and rest for ten minutes or so,' and proceeded to puke all over the grass.

'I think you might want to reconsider,' I said as he'd just started to roll a joint and looked like he was getting settled.

'Why man?' he said. His pallor by now was a deathly shade of yellow and grey and he definitely looked like he was on his last legs.

'Because I think the people who occupy this building might object to you puking on their nice grass and partaking of class C drugs on their premises.'

'Why? Whose building is it?' he muttered. Just then, his question was answered as a loud siren started to wail and a police cruiser swept out of the driveway in one hell of a hurry. I'm sure they had noticed Dave, but fortunately for both of us (as I was still in charge of the vehicle and was trying to get him out of the way for his own good as well as mine) they had more pressing business. Twenty minutes later we arrived at my home and thankfully his wife had turned up to drive him back to London. What a palaver! I swore from that point on to cautiously avoid all occasions where we might have to travel in the same vehicle as the smell was so bad in the car afterwards that I had to sell it. Poor old Dave. He still insists to this day, that his sickness and odd behaviour were brought about by eating a bad pie. Stupid boy!!

Apparently daft behaviour is not exclusive to the young; it works just as well for us old farts!

Chapter 48
The Nice 90s

During the 90s I kept very busy turning out six new albums, plus there were a host of re-issues. Not that I saw too much money from them, but the important thing was that it kept me and the band going and still out there doing what I do best: performing to live audiences. There were quite a few Jethro Tull conventions every year where either the Blods or just I made guest appearances. It was good fun and still continues to be, playing with Ian again as all old wounds real or imagined were healed in the due course of time. Even Glenn and I kissed and made up, deciding that life's too short to hold grudges.

Back in 1996 Ian very kindly graced me with his talent on an album called simply *One*. It was purely an acoustic album and Ian's excellent mandolin, harmonica and flute playing added a real cool texture to a few of the songs. It was done in a small studio in Buckingham and Ian's and my whole session was completed in just one evening. Great fun, and a very relaxed working vibe between us both existed on that project and I look forward to doing a bit more of the same at some point.

Two Blodwyn Pig albums came out in the 90's, the first being *Lies* in 1993, a good representation of the band at that time. We still keep a couple of numbers from that album in the set to this day, *Lies* being the most notable while *Deadman's Hill* has been a show closer for some time now. This album saw me return more to the roots of my playing, which is still very much steeped in rock and blues.

The truth about my playing and my whole thing about music in general is that I am very sponge-like, absorbing all styles of guitar playing and if anyone asks who my favourite player is (see the appendixes at the end of the book), I could name hundreds of musicians, but it would be very likely that the core of them would be blues players and especially the ones with a slight jazzy feel. There would be so many diverse players of all genres, as good, true feeling from the heart is of paramount importance to me and not necessarily the style. I just love everything from blues to all kinds of country picking to jazz, soul, classical and even some pop music if it is inventive and original. Who could deny that George Harrison was a true master of the most original and musical solos that anyone could ever hear. People like Eric Clapton just get better and more musical with age and maturity. I once had the ultimate privilege of sitting in with Herb Ellis, Oscar Peterson's guitarist and one of the world's greatest jazz players. He was a generous and brilliant musician who had influenced me greatly for many years and he was also an absolute gentleman. What a lovely guy.

I think nearly every British young guitar player in my formative years of playing must have bought the famous book *Play in a Day* by one of the country's foremost TV rock'n'roll performers and session guitarist, Bert Weedon. He must have started more guitar players off than anyone I know. It was then a great surprise when I visited a large local music store in my home town of Milton Keynes where Bert was doing an in-store demonstration and book signing session. It was my intention to go up to him and introduce myself and thank him for the kick start he gave me all those year ago. Instead of that happening I suddenly heard a voice behind me saying 'Hello, you're Mick Abrahams aren't you?' I turned around to be confronted by the smiling face of Bert, who shook my hand warmly and said how much he enjoyed my playing as he had heard some stuff that I'd done with all the various bands over the years.

To say the least, I was quite gobsmacked that someone like Bert would have even heard of me, let alone liked what I do! We ended up playing together at a charity bash in Stony Stratford which had been put together by Jim Marshall, the owner of Marshall Amplification and that was immense fun.

Chapter 49
Friends and Places Revisited

1996 was the year we recorded *Pig in the Middle* at Black Barn studios in Ripley Surrey, the birthplace and home territory of Eric Clapton. It was produced by an old pal, Robin Black, who as I mentioned earlier was the tape operator on the first Blodwyn Pig album, *Ahead Rings Out*. I had some good songs prepared for this project and it's still one of my favourites. Robin is such a nice guy and a consummate professional and I think he did a sterling job of the whole album from start to finish. I like to work in a happy atmosphere but with a focused attitude and, although there were a good few laughs and piss-taking in general, the whole thing got finished with the absolute minimum of stress.

There were two events that occurred around this time. The first was a very sad time especially for our good mate and drummer, Graham Walker. Jackie Challoner, Graham's wife and our backing singer (a great vocalist in her own right), suddenly found out that she had breast cancer and within nine months she passed away. She is still greatly missed as she was a truly gifted vocalist and a very lovely lady.

The second event was that Dave Lennox left the band to concentrate on Irish music and seeing how much more dope he could smoke! I had pondered the possibilities of going back to being a three-piece band and so Dave leaving the band made up my mind. He, of course, went with our best wishes and we still see him at gigs every now and then and he even turned up at my 60th birthday five years ago and unbelievably he wasn't even stoned! Well, not much really.

The 90s for me was a good overall time and during the latter part of 1996, just before Dave left the band, we were doing one of the by now regular Jethro Tull conventions, this time in Altenkirchen, Germany. It was a great night as usual and Ian made a guest appearance with the Blods and things went swimmingly. After the show we were all in the hotel bar having a good old session and generally putting the world to rights, telling gags and stories and having fun until the early hours of the morning. All the guys from the Tull fan magazine, *A New Day*, were there and there was a lot of talk about why didn't I put together a band to do some of the original numbers that we played from the first Tull album, *This Was*, as every time the band or I attended one of these gigs, we ended up doing a lot of the old songs from that era.

A lot a folks had been constantly nagging me to put something together like this, but I'd never given it much serious consideration up until this night, when the guys from the magazine started enthusing about such a project. After returning to England the next week, I started to think that this may not be such a bad idea. Maybe a one-off tour would be fun and I started to think about who might fit the bill. I searched around for a flute player band singer that could do the job without being too much of an obvious Ian Anderson lookalike, as I didn't want it to be a tribute band type of affair. For me, this was simply a walk down memory lane and a chance for the fans to get a glimpse of what the original line-up might have been like. Remember there are lots of Tull fans who weren't around when the original band was in existence, so for them it would a unique experience.

I was very lucky to be recommended to a guy who was currently playing in a Tull cover band called Seismic Ring and, having listened to him at a gig in Lincolnshire where they supported us, I stood at the side of the stage and closed my eyes and to me he sounded just like the very early Ian Anderson. Fortunately when I opened my eyes he didn't look at all like Ian, which was just what I wanted. His name was Steve Dundon and he was just six months old when we recorded This Was, a point which every night on stage, I never let him forget! A really talented and likeable lad with a great sense of humour, so he fitted in perfectly.

It would have been nice to have Clive to fill the drum stool, but he was committed elsewhere for most of the tour and, although he did play a couple of the last dates with us, he really wasn't very positive about the whole thing. Paul Burgess, who coincidentally had done a stint with Tull back in the late eighties and was also the drummer for the legendary 10cc, fitted in perfectly and is a very solid drummer. We nicknamed him Big Bird because of his big, awkward, gangly look and mannerisms. Mike Summerfield from the Blods took the bass spot and did a superb job all around.

The tour was only 32 dates and only took in the UK and with a couple of exceptions they were all great gigs and immensely enjoyable. I called the band the This Was Band as we were playing just the music from that album. My take on the whole thing was that I wanted to keep the original feel of the music, but with a modern approach to it. I knew it would never have the original rawness of the first band but I tried to improve on the arrangements and presentation in general with a couple of extra numbers that we did play with Tull back then but only occasionally. So the This Was Band it became and as a single project I felt it went well. We even did a live album compiled from some of the best of the gigs and called it *This Is*. Of course there were a few really annoying hiccups along the way, the first being the way in which it was advertised, which was blatantly abused by some of the less scrupulous promoters of the venues and I have to think that the information that was passed on to some of them by the agent might have been ambiguous too. The tour should have been advertised as "Mick Abrahams presents an evening of the music of Jethro Tull featuring the This Was Band" and that is what I clearly stated to the agency who booked it. This was because we were not a tribute band for the very simple fact that I am a founder member of the band and I am still living and working as an occasional guest member.

Also I didn't want to give the impression that I was trying to do a second-rate Tull with me at the helm. So I was gutted when I found out after about four gigs into the tour that further along in the tour some of the aforementioned less scrupulous promoters had done such snide tricks as advertising the concerts as "Mick Abraham's Jethro Tull" and even had it printed on the tickets! The posters on some of the venues had the name Jethro Tull first in huge letters and my name in much smaller lettering.

Chapter 50
Confusion, He Says

Needless to say it did cause some confusion with the fans who, when they rang up the venues to see if it was Jethro Tull that was appearing, the box office staff who were not clued up about the promotional cock-up and scheming promoters, simply assumed that it *was* Tull and said, 'Yes, that's what it says on the posters and tickets so it must be right.' The first time I had any inkling that there were a few dodgy deals being done behind my back with the ads I immediately tried put a stop to it, and said that if the ads were not presented as I had ordered then the tour would be cancelled! In fairness it was only about four dodgy promoters (and I won't name and shame them, but the cheeky scheming bastards know who they are and they can go screw themselves!).

Unfortunately, some damage had been done and through the Tull grapevine it got back to Ian and his eager solicitors (I think eager to bill him for the ever-growing complications they and a few shit stirrers were making). We carried on the tour, however, and ended up playing to some very appreciative crowds and the general opinion was that overall it was a great success. *A New Day* magazine (which has always been highly supportive of me) did a survey and 75% thought it was great and would like to see it happen again. 20% said they did like it a lot but were not happy about the way it was promoted (I agree with them, but what can you do? Just let everyone down and be a quitter? I think not!) and 5% simply hated it and wrote all sorts of shitty, whingeing letters to Ian and anyone who would listen about the fact that I was besmirching the good name of Tull and stuff like that. Didn't I know that I was not a member of Tull anymore and therefore not a founder member ... blah blah blah? To them I say this. It's your choice not to like it and that's fair enough, but I am a founder member by the simple fact I'm still living. I'm perfectly entitled to have done what I did and I am still proud of the music because that is what counts for me and not all the political bollocks. I am sorry if it offended the more sensitive of the fans who perhaps didn't even realise that Tull were founded in 1967 when they didn't know or even care about us or perhaps were not even born.

To them I say this. Go and moan at someone who deserves moaning at, like the dodgy promoters, lawyers, agents. The aforementioned whingers even started lobbying the magazine and that was really unhelpful and so in a way it turned the blame for all the problems around on me and the band, which to my mind was a real cop-out. I always try not to be involved in petty politics and squabbles, especially as I value the fans' input greatly and thank them for their support. I was a bit put out by this pettiness as I did what I did with good intentions and to give the fans what they had been asking to hear for quite a while and as it really was just a handful of moaners and not the majority I am happy that no serious damage was done.

An incident at the Glasgow Playhouse summed it up for me. We were playing to a near full house. In the middle of *Cat's Squirrel* sometimes young Steve would go and stand quietly and unobtrusively somewhere in the audience and on this occasion he had found a spot by one of the pillars at the back of the theatre. The crowd was stamping their feet, clapping wildly and even standing on the seats. A very miserable-looking guy singled poor Steve out and sidled up to him and said in a broad Glasgwegian brogue, 'I just hope you realise that there's a whole lot of people here tonight that are no' happy!'

Steve was gobsmacked and said, 'If they're not happy what the fuck are they all doing clapping and cheering and standing on the seats? A fucking Scottish rain dance, you pathetic dickhead?' Fair play to Steve, because he's only a small guy and I think he had a lot of balls coming up with that one. But the guy truly deserved it and I think if he'd had said it to me I might well have been inclined to kick his stupid arse.

At the end of it all I was pleased and relieved that we had got an overall great response from the fans and I had countless emails and letters from folks who said it was one of the best things I'd done for a while and it was a great trip down memory lane for them. Ian and I remain friends still and I think he realised, although he did give it his blessing in the first place, he had been misled into believing that the whole of the tour was badly advertised. The saying "You make love to just one sheep" comes to mind! I hope his solicitors didn't charge him too much for all that hard work they must have done! Forgive the sarcasm, but solicitors aren't my favourite animals! I know I've harped on a bit about dodgy promoters, agents, managers, accountants and solicitors. I have not got a problem with the decent and fair folks who do these jobs, as I know we have to have them and there are many more good ones than bad. I have no bitterness either towards them as a whole. As you can probably tell, I have fallen foul of some of the dodgy ones and, as life shows you, one or two rotten ones give all the others a bad name. It's a crying shame but there it is. I sincerely hope even the bad ones have mended their ways and started enjoying life and I wish them peace and happiness too.

Chapter 51
Health Problems.
2000: The First Operation

Around 1999 I was suffering increasingly from two sorts of physical pain. My right hand was constantly seizing up and going completely numb accompanied by excruciating pain in my arm and fingers. This was definitely a set-back as I couldn't even pick up my guitar without jagged bolts of pain ensuing and clearly something had to be done about it. The doctor told me I had a condition called Carpal Tunnel Syndrome in both of my hands, but more pronounced in the right. I needed to see a specialist. The good old NHS had a waiting list of a year! No way could I endure this for another year and looked into my meagre savings (I'd been saving up a few meagre pounds for contingencies just like this) and found that the cupboard was empty.

I was in panic and very pissed off and scared to be honest, as I wouldn't be able to even scrape a living if I couldn't play. I sunk into a depression and wondered what the heck I could do. I spoke to a friend who was, like me, a long-time member of the Musicians' Union and he suggested contacting the Musicians' Benevolent Fund. I got in touch with them and they were very sympathetic to my plight and funded everything and even arranged for me to go into a private clinic and have a minor operation to put the situation right. Amazing! Within one week I had had the consultation, was operated on within three days, recuperated for six weeks and was working again after two months - fantastic! I will eventually have to have the other hand seen to at some point, but up till now it has not given me too much trouble. I am eternally grateful to the caring and hard-working folks at the Musicians' Benevolent Society for their help.

The second pain – in my stomach - occurred in 2002, but it had been bothering me for a couple of years. I had put on a fair amount of weight over the years even though I was (and still am) exercising regularly and only doing what could be best described as social drinking. I would sometimes be doubled over, racked with pain and vomiting and feel generally like a train wreck. Again something clearly had to be done about it and this was only a short while after my first minor operation. It was now early 2003 and it had got to the point where once again I couldn't work as I never knew when an attack was imminent and it was really crippling.

Once again The Musicians' Benevolent Society came to my rescue and sent me off to a private clinic for tests and such like. I was diagnosed with gallstones and advised to have my gall bladder removed. This was a more major operation and it scared the living crap out of me, but the kindly surgeon assured me that all would be well. These days the operation is done mostly laparoscopically and there shouldn't be too much scarring or after effects. I was also amazed when he asked me when I would like to come in and have the procedure done. My lovely Kate was sitting with me holding my hand and keeping me calm and spoke up for me. 'When can you do it?' she asked.

'How about in two days' time?' he said.

'That'll be perfect,' said Kate.

It just didn't give me time to think but, what the heck, just go for it, I thought. And I said meekly, 'OK, that'll be fine.'

The operation was carried out successfully and as I was coming round from the anaesthetic, the surgeon, Robin Souter, a very nice guy with a great professional, calming manner who had 20 years' experience of this procedure, popped in to see that all was well and asked how I was feeling. Apart from being a bit sleepy I couldn't believe my ears when he told me this story. He said that, although the operation was a complete success, there were a few moments when he and his surgical team thought that they might have to abandon the laparoscopic route and open me up completely, which is a lot more messy and complicated.

The reason was that my gall bladder was rather large and inflamed and therefore difficult to pull through the small hole that it was intended to come through. They had just about given up on that when with one final tug it came out. Now here's where it gets freaky and amusing (well it was amusing after the event!). When they got the now redundant organ out and inspected it, Mr. Souter told me, it was shaped like a guitar and he did a rough drawing to prove his point. He said that in all the time he'd been doing this, he had never seen a gall bladder come out of someone's body in this shape. It made for a good few after dinner stories, I can tell you, and I asked him if they had kept it for posterity so that I could have it in a glass jar full of formaldehyde as a keepsake - maybe even to send it to the *Guinness Book of Records*: a guitar player with a gall bladder shaped like a guitar. Alas, they threw it away with all the other removed bits and pieces from various patients' bodies, so sadly I could claim no fame on that count, but it's an absolutely true story and it could have only happened to me!

Chapter 52
Birthday Bash

After the brief hospitalization I was thrown a surprise 60th birthday party by my dear missus, who gathered lots of family and friends to jump out on me at a pub where I thought we were just calling in at for a quick drink en route to a posh restaurant for a quiet dinner. She had been planning this for some time and this is one of the reasons that she was so quick to speak out about the timing of my gall bladder operation. She wanted me to be fully well and recovered by my birthday so that we could all enjoy ourselves without the risk of me suddenly being ill. It was an incredible night and in my typical quick sarcastic humoristic style, the moment when I walked unsuspectingly into the dimly-lit room and everyone shouted Happy Birthday, I stood there with a fake look of thunder on my face and said: 'What are you bastards all doing here? I don't like any of you, so bugger off and let me have a quiet drink!'

Thankfully it didn't work and they all stayed until the early hours and as John, our bass player, had got the key to my music studio from Kate earlier that day, he had collected all the stuff he figured I would need to play and set it up alongside a load of other various band instruments. My old pal Nigel 'Nobby' Neill had installed a PA for the event and we ended up with a great night full of music and fun with lots of guys from my past suddenly turning up and blowing. Fantastic: just a good evening's fun and that's how it should be! I didn't get any grub though because I was so busy talking and playing that I omitted to notice the buffet in another room and by the time midnight was upon us it had all been scoffed! I did get a packet of crisps from behind the bar though so things weren't so bad.

Chapter 53
Looking Back From Now

It's now 2008 as I am finishing this account of my life in music and its twists and turns. I will have passed my 65th birthday in April by the time this account is published (and hopefully being read by millions of people). And there are so many great things happening this year that it promises to be my busiest year for a while now. Over the last couple of years gigs have not been as forthcoming as they have been in the past, and to be honest I'm not bothered about trudging out every other day to gigs. I just choose when and where I want to play and spend a lot of my time writing and composing and doing the odd session for other projects.

In 2003 I did something which I had been meaning to do but had been putting off for some time and finally became a Freemason, which is one of the best decisions I have made. I belong to two Lodges, one known as my Mother Lodge (the Lodge where I was first initiated into Freemasonry), Chelsea Lodge Number 3098, whose members are musicians and guys associated with the entertainment industry in general. We meet at Freemasons Hall in Great Queen Street, London, which is also the home of the United Grand Lodge of England and we have a great time every time we meet. We also do the Chelsea Road Show which raises funds for various charities and worthy causes and it is immensely rewarding to entertain the brethren of the various lodges up and down the country and the general public too and to know that what we do is truly worthwhile.

I am also a member of a local Lodge, Brickhill Lodge

number 6968, which is near to my home and the members there are from mixed backgrounds and trades. It is also (as all Freemasons Lodges are) a great Lodge for charity fund raising and the fellowship again is wonderful. I have made many new friends since joining Freemasonry and have been constantly very pleasantly surprised to find just how many guys that I have known for some time are brothers too. I feel like I am part of a universally spread brotherhood and as I was brought up as an only child it feels like a great big extended family. As a believing Christian and a member of a church it has also helped my faith to grow. The strange thing about Freemasonry is that it comes under criticism from extreme groups in some churches, but for me there is absolutely no conflict as Freemasonry is definitely not a religion and does not purport to be so. It is about morality, growth and strength of character.

I feel I am answerable to God first, family and friends second and lastly Freemasonry, so I am certain that I have my priorities in the right order. This is borne out by the fact that many Christian ministers as well as senior members of other faiths are Freemasons. It has no racial or religious boundaries and is open to men of all faiths over 21 and of good character. And that is something I most definitely agree with. Just as a footnote it should be pointed out that, although it is a Brotherhood, there are ladies who have their own Lodges, so the girls get a bit of a turn too, but us guys are not allowed into their Lodge meetings, nor they into ours. My friend's wife and I were discussing this very subject one night at dinner and I asked her how she felt about my mate and me going off to Lodge meetings where women were not allowed in. She put it very simply and amusingly too. 'No, I don't care a hoot! Do you think we would let you lot join the Women's Institute? I think not!'

Also it's the one way that I feel that I can give something back for all the wonderful gifts I have been given in form of the capability to play and entertain and the love, from my family and innumerable friends who have seen me through good and hard times and have always remained steadfast in every way.

For information about Chelsea Lodge number 3098 you can refer to a book called *That's Entertainment* compiled by Keith Skues (yes, that's The Keith Skues from pirate radio and BBC fame), which gives a fascinating look into the history of the Lodge and a list of members past and present dating back to 1905. I am certain you will be pleasantly surprised in recognising some very famous entertainers and celebrities from every sphere of show business. I feel honoured to be in such good company; and naturally very proud to follow in the footsteps of some of my greatest childhood heroes.

Chapter 54
The Interim Albums and DVDs

Throughout 2001 and 2002 I concentrated on writing, recording and producing more albums. The first one that I finished was *See My Way*, which included a remake of two of the most popular Blodwyn Pig songs, the title track *See My Way* and a new version of *Dear Jill*. Back in 1969 this song was released as a single as well as making an appearance on the Ahead Rings Out album. I loved it then and I still do. It was included in a movie called Almost Famous (just a bit like me!), which was produced by Cameron Crowe, a great producer. It was made and bank rolled by Dream Works, the mighty Steven Spielberg's company. I was chuffed to say the least and had naïve day dreams of suddenly for once in my life actually making a whole lot of money out of the deal.

Guess what? The film did fairly well in the US and it was mildly successful through Europe, but as the song writers' union in the states had capitulated to the movie giants over the way royalties were to be paid out a long time back, there were no royalties to be had from the song appearing in the film, just a one-off fee and that was that! The rest of the world apparently does pay royalties pro rata for each time the film is shown but not the USA. To finally dash my hopes of buying my first Aston Martin, the song was not included on the sound track CD. I would have received much more money had it done so. I'm not whining Because, at the end of the day, I did get a payout but it was minute compared to what might have been! Hey ho, that's life. At least I got something and you know what they say. 10% of something is better than

100% of nothing and at least I got one of my songs in a movie.

The next album was a boxed set of various songs that I had compiled over the last few years and had archived up until 2002. It was called *All Said and Done* and included music from the This Was Band tour and some studio songs. As a bonus there is a DVD interview with the erstwhile writer and musician Martin (Jet) Celmins lasting for around an hour. I had also been approached to do a live DVD with my regular band Graham Walker on drums and John 'Guinness' Gordon on bass. We chose one of my favourite small blues club venues, the Half Moon at Bishop's Stortford, a very down-home and vibrant club run by a lovely chap by the name of Richard Pavitt. We had an absolute ball doing it and it gave me a chance to play all the styles that I like most. So first we had a a unplugged set as they call it (and I really don't know why they call it that, because we were all plugged in but with electro-acoustic guitars!)

The second set consisted of just the band playing a full electric set, which was really cool and very musical. As it's a very intimate type of venue it also gave me the chance to have a good laugh with the audience, many of whom I know quite well by now. I was told that the whole thing would be edited – blah, blah - but guess what? They lied to me again! The opening shot of us coming onstage hears me saying to the audience, 'Don't worry, folks. If we fuck anything up tonight, we can always do another version because they are editing it all later!' They didn't edit it at all, which in a way is a good thing because there wasn't any needed on the music. It did, however, show the rather mischievous and colourful side of my gags and anecdotes, but I know the audience loved it, so no worries. The only thing that surprised me a little was the fact that they then told me it was going out to some of the bigger main retailers like ASDA, Our Price. Woolworths and Tesco. Oh well, I had already done the deal so there wasn't much I could do about it but it did make me think that some innocent 10 year-old might have got the DVD in his or her Christmas stocking and asked his or her parents: 'What's "fuck it all up" mean? Why did that funny guitar bloke tell a story about why ladies don't fart? (Bad news, kid: you've been lied to. Ladies fart a lot better than men; they're just better than us at covering it up by coughing loudly!).

That's perhaps me being old-fashioned and maybe it's all part and parcel of the way things are today. And given my statements about my naivety at the age of 10 maybe it's not so surprising after all. That's me though: mouth first, brain second, but I do like making people laugh as well as playing music because I am an entertainer and that's what entertainers do! So there it is. If you've bought it you can edit out the bits you don't want with the computer software that's available today. The DVD does continue to be popular and although I did sell it out directly to the film company as a one-off (story of my life), I think it has sold well, so job done, move on.

Chapter 55
Back With The Blues Again, Can't Stop Now and the Doomsday Clock

I should have mentioned that back during 1996/7 there was a very odd project that I was involved with called *The Doomsday Clock*. It was an off-beat and surreal opera written by a lovely chap by the name of Mark Law. Mark (a highly intellectual type of guy with a good sense of humour) was totally obsessed with Albert Einstein and an Orwellian vision of a world decimated by nuclear weapons and he wrote a whole batch of songs based around this vision. He recruited me and Clive Bunker and our old mate Jim Rodford from the Kinks and the Zombies to be the mainstay of the rhythm section and brought in other players and singers to complete the work. It gave me a chance to do my Mad McGregor voice as one of the songs, *Train Ride to Hell*, had dear old McGregor driving his nightmare locomotive and doing his thing. I had a lot of fun doing this and although I played guitar on the entire track I really enjoyed the acting aspect of it (doing the character was very much about acting rather than singing). Mark was so impressed with my ability to sing and act the part of a total psycho that he asked me to do a couple more, namely the part of Boris the evil arms dealer from hell and Albert, one of the NIMBYs (not in my back yard). The only criticism I could raise was that a lot of the songs were in a minor key and ended up at times sounding a bit like a Yiddish wedding where some bright spark had dropped LSD in the punchbowl! It was different and we all had a great time doing it.

The most recent of my work is *Mick's Back With the Blues Again*. It's a no-frills CD of some time-tested standard blues songs with a few of my originals thrown in for good measure. Everything I play has always come out with blues at the very heart of it, although I don't consider myself a blues purist. I am what I like to think of as a bit of a mongrel player, a bit of this and a bit of that. But at least it's me and I guess, good or bad, you can be the judge of that. It's original and it's me because it's the only way I know how to do it! Having the sense of humour that I do, I can't resist writing the odd song here and there with a bit of micky taking and you will find a song on this album with a reference to my being fed up with having to take so many pills and stuff for various aches, pains, ills and chills (mostly associated with growing older!), but with a verse which refers to the impending trip to the old folks' home (I really don't want to go!) with the line: I'm even hearing Mantovani records! I wrote this verse whilst drooling just to give it that touch of authenticity! Only kidding, folks, and certainly no insult intended to folks older than me, who are becoming fewer by the week.

On the album *Can't Stop Now* you can hear the verses of the song *GBNHS Blues* starting off with 'Woke up this morning there were curtains all round my head', which referred to the last visit I made to our local hospital with some strange infection which completely flattened me. The people who work in these places should be given a medal for the crap they have to put up with from the way the NHS is organised and funded. These days it is woefully inadequate and I am not being political as I tend to think that, with a few remarkable exceptions, my experience of politicians is that sadly a lot of them are total liars and self-promoting dickheads.

Chapter 56
Different Strokes

Two albums that I am very proud of are of music that would most certainly not be normally associated with me: *A Midsummer Night's Dream* and *How Many Times*. The first album was done initially as an album of background music for my son's school play of the same name in which he appeared at the age of 12. It was all a bit incestuous in the sense that the Headmistress and my wife Kate (who is now the deputy head) asked me to provide the music and I was happy to oblige. What to do was the burning question for me, but I very quickly got my head around the project and came up with some original themes and songs to accompany the production. My son Nick was playing the part of Oberon, the crafty fairy prince, so I wrote a song specifically for him and it seemed to take on a life of its own from that point. A couple of the other cast members wanted songs too and I duly obliged. Although it was an amateur production, it stood up rather well and of course it was a treat seeing my younger son being a part of the production, which made me and Kate very proud.

We thought it had just been consigned to the archive vault of One-Off Productions Ltd, but in 2002, by which time Nick had left the school and gone into visual design as a career, the school decided that the senior school drama group would revisit the play and once again called upon my services to update the music and write a few more songs for their production. This time it got a bit more serious as they planned to take it to the Edinburgh Festival and let the public see the new version. I took a bit more time with the writing and production as they had grander designs this time and were most definitely out to impress. I called on the help of a few good mates including the very talented Sharon Watson, who for a long time had done backing vocal work on some of my albums and who is an incredible vocalist in her own right. I also roped in another good pal, Paul Bell, who has a wonderful gravely soul type of voice which suited the occasion perfectly. The young actors ranged from 16 to 18 years and they did a fine job individually of the songs and the new remixed and enhanced production was really cool. They completed the week in Edinburgh to excellent reviews and everyone was very happy with the result.

I decided not to consign the production to my archive shelves and eventually replaced the actor's vocals with Sharon, Paul and myself taking the various characters' roles. I remixed it yet again with the new vocals and put it up on my website as a one-off project and collector's item. I was even more surprised when I got a call from Dr Ken Pickering, who is a musical director involved with Canterbury Cathedral and an avid Shakespeare authority and, as it turns out, a Jethro Tull and Blodwyn Pig fan. He is very keen to see the music being used in productions of the play when and wherever it might be merited, so I am keeping my fingers crossed!

The second album is called *How Many Times* and it's a collection of songs that I have written over a period of a few years and not got around to using on any of my albums. The reasons for this were I just couldn't sing them and do them any justice at all, or they weren't the type of songs that I would play but I really liked them as songs. After a chance conversation with Sharon Watson she said that, after listening to them, that it was a real pity that I didn't write songs like that for her! Sharon had been a singer in the number one band of the National Youth Jazz Orchestra at the incredibly young age of 14 years. To my mind she was more than qualified to do the songs justice. So I said; 'Well, why not give them a shot?' We went into the studio and within a week we had some pretty amazing vocals in the can. I was so impressed that I wrote a couple more for her to sing during the week that we were recording, including the title track *How Many Times*. It hasn't been taken up by any major record company so far but it is on sale from my website shop. I love Sharon's voice and it is a first for me to venture into a different realm of song writing not immediately related to rock or blues. It remains a firm favourite album of mine to this day.

Chapter 57
My Family and the Future

Although I am now 65 years old (my birthday was 7th April for those of you who may wish to donate large sums retrospectively or even small sums to help me in my impending dotage), there are lots of great things to look forward to. My elder son Alex, as I might have mentioned earlier, is a superb guitarist and has written and played some very beautiful songs and instrumentals. He is currently working on a new album with a band that he has put together and I am very optimistic about his future. I know that at some point we will do a whole project together when we both have the right timing sorted out with our respective schedules. Like his old man he has a quirky and surreal sense of humour and he is great and very entertaining to be with. My younger son Nick is a highly talented visual designer and works for one of the largest fashion chains in the world. He truly enjoys his work and is innovative and professional to a fault. It's a safe bet to say that he will just continue to rise higher and higher in his chosen profession because of his level of commitment. He's a great lad again with a wicked sense of humour and a great mate too. When the two of them are visiting Kate and me at the same time I don't think we ever stop having fun and I have to say that they've got me beat when it comes to having the craic. I can still talk the talk when it comes to it but I have to be helped to bed at times!

What can I say about my beautiful wife and best friend, Kate? We've been through a lot together and again we are still looking forward to a lot more together. She is the best wife and best mate anyone could have. I count myself extremely lucky and very blessed to have someone like her to share my life with. If it wasn't for her great loving and kind nature I would probably be lost! She is a great mum to Nick and a great friend to Alex and loves them both dearly. How she manages to put up with me and my funny ways I will never know, but according to her I brighten her life up too as she never knows what to expect from me and my wacky behaviour one day to the next. In this respect, it's an odd form of consistency. She says that she would rather have the roller coaster ride just like me because that way life is never dull and boring!

The extended families are simply brilliant. Kate has two brothers and one older sister who we all get on great with. Another shock to my system was when my mum died in May of 2007 at the age of 100. I had always known that I was an adopted child right from the age of six, as Mum and Dad told me in that kindly way that although I wasn't born to my mum, I was from somewhere else, but very much loved and wanted and to me this didn't seem to make one ounce of difference; so no problems there. Later in life, as I reflected on that revelation and how it might have affected me mentally, I came to the decision that things are just what they are meant to be and that's it!

I heard stories about how other folks in similar situations had wondered all their lives about where they originated from and why they were like they were. I never gave that too much attention either, but as I got older I started to become curious. I did make a promise to myself that I would never seek after information about my biological family until my adopted parents were either deceased or I was! I took this attitude because although my mum had offered many times to give me a piece of paper with the information on how to find out everything I might have wanted to know, I just couldn't bring myself to do it. As even though my Mum and I had our differences from time to time, I know that she loved me in her old-fashioned and Edwardian way (she came from a huge family of 14 children and had a seriously strict and hard upbringing) and didn't know any other way to deal with someone like me, who I think went against every grain of the way she'd been brought up. It was simply respect and duty: that's how I saw it.

My dad passed away a long time back in 1983 and so with Mum passing on I started to get a little more curious. I put the wheels in motion to search for my birth parents and after a couple of months came up with mostly false trails and misinformation and people just wanting to take my money for supposed "detective work". I have a good mate called Stuart who is an ex Met police detective and over a pint one evening I told him my dilemma. He just simply said, 'Here are some forms: just fill them in and sign them and I'll get some info for you.' Within a month I had some feedback from various government archives regarding adoptions, births etc and lo and behold I found a few clues as to my origins. Some of it was convoluted but I certainly found out who my biological mother was and where I was born. It also turned out happily that I have a younger half sister called Sharyn who lives in Delaware, USA, and here is a real freaky story, but it's 100% true.

Chapter 58
My New Sister

Kate and I had gone to visit some friends in Lowestoft, Suffolk, and we knew through some of the documentation that had been passed on to me that that was where my birth mother had lived during 1943. We had been doing some research in the local records library and it was getting toward lunch time and we were both tired and in need of some sleep before visiting our friends for a nice meal together that evening. I said: 'Let's get back to the hotel and grab some sleep for a couple of hours.' I called a cab and on the way back to the hotel I struck up a conversation with the driver. I asked him if he knew a certain street in the town as we had got the original address we were seeking from the library.

'It's just about 500 yards up there,' he pointed.

'Could you do us a favour, mate?' I asked, 'and just stop off in the street and wait for a minute or so; there's a house I want to see.'

'Sure,' he said and drove into the street. 'You're lucky that this road is still here,' he said. 'It's one of the few places that the Luftwaffe's bombs missed when they were busy malleting the docks in Lowestoft all those years ago during the Second World War!'

I got out of the cab and Kate sat quietly in the back looking at me. I very gingerly knocked on the door of the house number I had been given. I really didn't think for one minute that I would find anyone at home so I don't know what possessed me to do it. There was no answer; so I went to the house next door. Still there was no answer.

I was about to get back in the cab when Kate and the driver pointed to the house on the other side of the one where I had knocked. I shrugged and knocked on that door too. It opened up immediately; I think the lady who answered might have seen me knocking and wondered if I was either a burglar trying to nick her telly or a Jehovah's Witness seeking to save her soul.

'I'm sorry to trouble you, love,' I said politely, 'but I'm seeking information about someone who I have been told lived here a long time ago.'

'Who and when?' asked the lady.

'Molly Stuart.'

She inspected me with a quizzical look and said: 'Molly was my best friend's Mum. Who might you be?' I couldn't believe I was hearing this.

'I'm fairly certain she is my mother,' I said weakly. The lady nearly fainted with shock and steadied herself on the door frame.

'Well, I'm sorry to tell you that your mother passed away in the USA a long time back, but I have some news for you which should please you. My best friend Sharyn (Molly's second child by another marriage) is your sister!'

Again I couldn't believe my ears! This was a real shock to my system. I had not expected to find either of my blood parents still alive so the news that my mother was dead came as no great surprise; but to find out that I had a half sister was wonderful.

The kind lady who gave me the news was named Maria and she gave me Sharyn's address and contact details whilst I stood at the door. As she went back inside the house I could hear the radio playing Planet Rock and heard what I vaguely thought was familiar. As by now I had been standing at Maria's doorstep for nearly twenty minutes (she did ask me in; but I declined as I was nervous and said that I had a cab waiting), Kate came over to join me and we got into a long conversation.

The cab driver said: 'No problem. Mate. I'll wait as long as you need. Your wife has just been telling me about your search, so take your time.'

Maria told me that Sharyn had always known that she had an older brother out there somewhere and that she would be delighted to hear from me. She asked me what I did for a living and so I told her in a fairly matter of fact way that I was a long time professional guitar player and singer.

'Have you played with anyone that I might have heard of?' she asked and I told her about my band work and my origins with Jethro Tull. It was then that the amazing bit happened. She said 'Crikey! I am a big Tull fan, I must have seen you play at some point back in the 60s. In fact that's Jethro Tull playing on the radio right now and they played a Jethro Tull song just about the time that you were knocking at the next door house. In fact that day had had a programme dedicated to 60s progressive rock bands and Tull and Blodwyn Pig were featured heavily! I listened to the song from the front door and unbelievably it was *Beggars Farm* playing right at that very moment! How about that for freaky?

Chapter 59
New Contacts

I waited until we returned home the next day and just couldn't wait to ring up my new family member. It was very emotional talking to someone on the phone that you have never met - didn't realise existed. I have yet to meet Sharyn in the flesh but we talk regularly on the phone and by email and have sent each other videos and photos of our respective folks. I'm sure we will meet up sometime soon and I am really looking forward to that time. As for finding my biological father, well, that was another kettle of fish and a very confusing kettle too! It turned out that a gentleman called Alfred Warwick had married my birth mother in the latter part of 1943 but never laid claim to being my father. It looked to me like a case of someone very much in love in time of war who had a brief affair with my mother but maybe had just married her to make what they called in those days "an honest woman" out of her. Unfortunately the marriage didn't last for long and as I explained briefly earlier my wayward mother started up an affair with an American serviceman (there were lots of American and British military personnel posted all along that part of the country at that time) and in 1945 Sharyn was born.

Just like myself, she was put up for adoption, so I whilst I can't make any judgments about her reasons for doing the same thing twice in a row, I think in retrospect I am so very glad that my adopted mum and dad prevailed when all the tugging back and forth was going on, because I honestly feel that I got the best part of the deal. I have since been in touch with the Warwick family because there is a common link, albeit only the fact that Bob Warwick is Alfred Warwick's son by another marriage. I am looking forward to meeting up with him and his family at some point. I've spoken to him and his daughter Kim a few times and they seem like very decent and kind people. It must have come as a bit of a shock to their system to think that someone had just turned up out of the mists of time and said: 'I think your dad was my dad too!' We even went to the length of having DNA tests to see who was who, but it turned out that we were not linked by blood, only by a marriage certificate that confused us all.

I can only conclude from these events that whilst I know for a fact who my birth mother was, I don't know yet who my dad could have been. Like the old gag says, "my dad was some soldiers". Who knows? I don't know and now I don't particularly care as I don't want to spend the rest of my life living in a potential spy novel! Life's much more interesting without all that crap. Let it all calm down and await the next chapter, I think!

Chapter 60
The Best is Yet to Come

Like all musicians that have survived the rigours of a turbulent time over the years, I feel that my best work is yet to come. I have learnt a lot of good things from great people and great players alike and know now how to take a breath so to speak and leave a few gaps where they should be in the music. I've still got much to give and have no intention of doing this awful thing that some folk call retirement! I do still lead a very active life, what with doing a bit of shooting (clays, a few pheasants, vermin and the like). I visit the gym regularly and work out and swim, so I do lead a relatively healthy and positive lifestyle. I don't smoke at all and although I drink socially it's not often and again I guess I am lucky that I didn't get trapped by alcoholism and drug addiction like so many of my unfortunate fellow musicians and friends. The old saying, "there but for the Grace of God go I" is very apt in my case and for that I am eternally grateful. I couldn't think of not playing and entertaining; I just wouldn't know what to do with myself.

I am about to embark on a few more projects this year and am currently busy organising all the logistics leading up to my 65th birthday concert. At the same time I will be celebrating the 40th anniversary of Jethro Tull as well as Blodwyn Pig and by the time this book reaches the shops I will have performed as a special guest yet again with Ian Anderson and the current line up of Tull. The concert for my birthday bash will see a few very special guests of mine too and I'm hoping that of course Ian will reciprocate by doing me the honour of playing a couple of tunes with the Blods.

The DVD project about me and my history on film is going ahead whilst I am finishing this book and it will take the form of a lot of early footage of Blodwyn Pig and the Mick Abrahams Band and some interviews. There is a wealth of footage to sift through and currently the Bletchley College media group are taking great pains to get the work done. I have had a look at some of the personal video diaries from the road from around 1988 onwards. I just wish there had been personal video cameras available way back in the 60s and 70s but we've still got a few gems that were captured by certain folks who have sent in Super 8mm film, so it promises to be good.

I have also decided to incorporate a section which will run in tandem with some of the footage. I am always being quizzed about various licks and chord structuring that is peculiar to my own brand of playing, so I thought, well, when there is a number that is shown during the footage, why not at the end actually show the relevant part and how I play it? And also have a guitar student right there alongside me in the studio and show him and the people who buy the DVD how it's done. I think it is a workable idea and I hope that it will encourage up and coming players how to develop an individual approach to playing guitar in general. The last part of the DVD (which looks increasingly like it will be a double DVD by the time we are done!) will be a complete record of the concert and the party, possibly with some interviews. And, knowing me and my pals, there will certainly be some fairly rich out-takes from the whole project which we will include, warts and all!

Chapter 61
The Last Word

I will close the pages on this book by saying just how grateful I am to have lived such a rich and diverse life, even though some of it has been harrowing. But hopefully it will continue for a while to come. The fact that these days I am not the man described truthfully during the earlier parts of the book is a testament to the fact that I have a solid faith in God and confidence in myself - and that is God's doing, not mine - a wonderful loving family, brothers, sisters and friends beyond compare all over the world.

I am probably not the easiest person to live with at times and I am acutely aware of my own shortcomings. But I have always stayed true to what I do, what I am and what I play. I like to think I am a very honest person, perhaps sometimes to the point of being far too blunt; but that's me. Take it or leave it. So to all who read my story, the friends and fans especially, I thank you all and hope you receive as much good fortune and as many blessings as I have. I couldn't fit everyone's names into the story so instead I have made a list in the indexes of the book of your names. If I have missed you out, please don't think I don't remember you. Just put it down to senior moments as I am now a senior!

Thank you and God bless you always.

Mick Abrahams 2008

Appendix

My 102 Favourite Guitar Players (in alphabetical order):

1. Albert Collins
2. Albert King
3. Albert Lee
4. Alex Abrahams
5. Alexis Korner
6. Andrés Segovia
7. Angus Young
8. B B King
9. Barney Kessel
10. Bert Jansch
11. Bert Weedon
12. Big Bill Broonzy
13. Blind Lemon Jefferson
14. Blind Reverend Gary Davis
15. Bo Diddley
16. Bob Brozman
17. Bobby Parker
18. Bonnie Rait
19. Brian Jones
20. Bruce Welch
21. Buddy Emmons
22. Buddy Guy
23. Charlie Christian
24. Chet Atkins
25. Chuck Berry
26. Davy Graham
27. Dennis Greaves
28. Derek Trucks

29. Dierdre Cartwright
30. Django Reinhardt
31. Doc Watson
32. Dolly Parton
33. Duane Allman
34. Eddie Van Halen
35. Edgar Winters
36. Elliott Randall
37. Eric Clapton
38. Eric Snow
39. Frances Rossi
40. Freddie King
41. Geoff Whitehorn
42. George Benson
43. George Harrison
44. Gerry Reed
45. Gordon Huntley
46. Hank Marvin
47. Herb Ellis
48. Huddie Leadbetter (Leadbelly)
49. James Burton
50. Jeff Beck
51. Jerry Douglas
52. Jimi Hendrix
53. Jimmy Page
54. Jimmy Vaughn
55. Joe Pass
56. John Martyn
57. John Renbourn
58. John Williams
59. Johnny (Guitar) Watson
60. Johnny Smith
61. Johnny Winter

62. Julian Bream
63. Keith Richards
64. Les Paul
65. Lightnin Hopkins
66. Lloyd Green
67. Lonnie Johnson
68. Lucky Peterson
69. Martin Barre
70. Martin Taylor
71. Matt (Guitar) Murphy
72. Merle Travis
73. Mick Mckay
74. Mississippi Fred Mcdowell
75. Otis Rush
76. Paul Kossoff
77. Pete Townsend
78. Pete Wilsher
79. Rhet Stoller
80. Richard Thompson
81. Rick Parfitt
82. Ricky Scaggs
83. Robben Ford
84. Robbie Robertson
85. Robert Cray
86. Robert Johnson
87. Robin Trower
88. Roy Buchanan
89. Ry Cooder
90. Scotty Moore
91. Sister Rosetta Tharpe
92. Son House
93. Sonny Landreth
94. St Louis Jimmy

95. Stefan Grossman

96. Steve Cropper

97. Stevie Ray Vaughn

98. Tal Farlow

99.   Walter Trout

100. Wes Montgomery

101. Willie Nelson

102. Woody Guthrie

Acknowledgements

To Kate Abrahams. Nick Abrahams. Alex Abrahams. For their unfailing love and support in everything I have ever done and for being the best family anyone could possibly have.

To Martin Turner for encouragement and help beyond the call of duty, for friendship and helping me believe I could actually write this book!

Martin Webb and Dave Rees and all at *A New Day* magazine for being constantly supportive and helpful.

Jeff Adams. For his superb harmonica.

Ian Anderson. For helping my steps take right direction and friendship.

Andrea Bandi. For Friendship.

Dave Bedford. For Friendship and making sure I never ran the London Marathon!

Paul Bell. For Friendship and a great voice.

Clive Bunker. For Friendship and great drumming.

Peter Brend. For Friendship and support.

David Copperfield. For Friendship and keeping me laughing!

Rachal Davidson. For all the hard work on current projects.

Richard Desmond. For Friendship and letting me beat him at squash!

Ritchie Dharma. For Friendship and great drumming.

Steve Dundon. For Friendship and great flute playing.

Pete Fensome. For Friendship and great bass playing.

Andrea Garavelli. For Friendship and great bass playing.

John (Guinness) Gordon. For Friendship and great bass playing.

Ralph Goss. For Friendship and great drinking ability!

211

Colin Hodgkinson. For Friendship and great bass playing.

Brian Hodgson. For Friendship and great bass playing.

Alex Hold. For Friendship and great roadying all these years!

Bob (bombardier) Jenkinson. For Friendship and just being a Gunner!

Paul (cabbage hat) Buchanan for friendship and cool photography.

Paul Jones. For Friendship and great harmonica playing and being an all-round good guy.

Julianna Rhodes. For Friendship support.

Alexis Korner. For Friendship and being a great influence in my life.

Jools Kendall. For Friendship and support.

Hillary Kiff. For Friendship and support.

Chris Lambrianou. For Friendship and support.

Jack Lancaster. For Friendship and great musicianship.

Albert Lee. For Friendship and being a great influence.

Sue Lindars. For Friendship and support.

Pete Lindars. For Friendship and support.

Sara McCarthy. For Friendship and support and making sure my body still works!

Les Minney. For Friendship and support.

Pete Moody. For Friendship and support.

Nigel (Nobby) Neill. For Friendship and support.

Kimbo Neill. For Friendship and support.

Andy Pyle. For Friendship and great bass playing.

Elliott Randall. For Friendship and great guitar playing.

Jim Rodford. For Friendship and great bass playing.

Steve Rodford. For Friendship and great drumming.

Dexter Smith. For chopping my dogs up.

Mike Summerland. For great bass playing and eating my toothpaste!

Andy Viccars. For Friendship and making sure my guitars

work properly.

Graham Walker. For Friendship and great drumming.

Sharyn Warwick.For Friendship and being my new sister!

Sharon Watson. For Friendship and great singing.

Geoff Whitehorn.For Friendship and great guitar playing.

Frank Lea. For friendship and support.

Rikki Massini. For friendship and great guitar playing.

If I have missed anyone out, I am truly sorry but it's not because I think any the less of you or have forgotten you. It's just that I really need a cup of tea and I'm tired!

www.apexpublishing.co.uk